Catskill
Rambles

Catskill
Rambles

KENNETH WAPNER

THE OVERLOOK PRESS
Woodstock • New York

First published in 1992 by
The Overlook Press
Lewis Hollow Road
Woodstock, New York 12498

Library of Congress Cataloging-in-Publication Data

Wapner, Kenneth
  Catskill rambles / Kenneth Wapner.

     p. cm.

   1. Catskill Mountains (N.Y.)—Description and travel. I. Title.

F127.C3W36   1991
974.7'38—dc20   91-27932
                                                          CIP
                                                           AC

ISBN: 0-87951-442-6

CONTENTS

WILD
CATSKILL GINSENG

SHAWN SPANHAKE IS thirty-three years old—a big man with blond hair, clipped mustache, and wary blue eyes. The morning I met him outside his rented trailer in Pine Hill he was dressed in camouflage pants, a blue-shirt, woodsman boots, and a camouflage cap. We shook hands, and Spanhake asked again how I'd found him.

It was a curious story; I'd hooked up with Spanhake in a roundabout way. Steve Witte, owner of the Colonial Inn in Pine Hill, happened to have mentioned that he had plans to hunt ginseng with Jan Czajka. I hadn't been aware that ginseng grows wild in the Catskills. The quest had an instant appeal. Witte told me to call Czajka. When I reached him, he hedged about ginseng, but said I was welcome to tag along fishing. I joined him outside his trailer by the train tracks in Phoenicia early one morning. Taking both cars, we sped west to the portal in Shandaken.

Czajka has a thick Polish accent and loves to talk almost as much as he loves to fish. He grew up in the mountains on the Czech-Pole border and said he spent much of the war slaving in a Nazi labor camp. He came to this country after the war and until retirement worked on tugs from the Gulf of Mexico to Nova Scotia. As we assembled our gear he launched into fishing stories set in the Carpathian Mountains. In one, he elaborately acted out spearing a twenty-pound brown trout with a pitchfork. He danced in the roadside gravel, mimicking his struggles with the enormous fish he'd once impaled.

The sun was still behind the ridges when we made our way down to the water. Czajka fished salmon eggs, and I dry flies, which he assured me were a waste of time. He was right, of course. I had hooked one small fish by the time the sun finally hit the water just before eight. Czajka lobbed his rig into a back eddy and let it drift downstream where the warmer portal water churned. In this manner he pulled in five keepers, one a fat, thirteen-inch brown.

We tried several other spots with the same results. Occasionally, black-and-silver arrows flashed under my fly. Once a bullet-nose struck, but either I was too slow or the hook didn't take. The sun rose two fists in the sky, and I slid through the currents in sneakers and shorts. Czajka was in heaven—every other cast was a strike. When he hooked a fish, a beatific smile spread across his face. He looked like a boy reeling them in.

Between fishing spots I asked him again about ginseng. "I hunt it every once in a while," he said. "Just a little bit. For myself."

I'd heard he'd found $800 worth the year before.

"Naw." He shook his head and chuckled. "My ankle! She no good," he said in his lilting voice. He'd twisted it just a few days prior. Ginseng hunting was out of the question.

"Oh shit!" I heard him yell later that morning. He approached me limping, a sorry expression on his face.

Before we parted, Czajka gave me his fish and rummaged through a 4 x 6-inch plastic snap box stuffed with hundreds of flies. He picked out two nymphs and one streamer and told me to match them at the local sporting goods store. He also suggested that I contact Spanhake about ginseng.

I called Spanhake that evening; he was guarded on the phone. The ginseng berries were ripe, and tomorrow was a legal picking day. I could come along. "I hope you're in shape," he added as we hung up.

That was how I found myself in Spanhake's car talking local genealogy on our way to the hunt. Spanhake's grandfather had come from Germany and settled in the Wittenberg Valley. Nearly everyone in the family had at one time worked for Nelson Shultis, who we both agreed was a pisser.

"He'll eat anything that moves. Snapping turtle is his favorite food. You didn't know that?" Spanhake was incredulous, as though I had missed the essential aspect of the man.

We discussed local ginseng (which Spanhake, Czajka, and Witte pronounced "*gin*-shang"). Wild Catskill ginseng was top-grade and sold for three times the amount of the cultivated variety. There was a large market in New York City. That year the root was bringing $225 a dry pound. Spanhake mostly sold it wet; he didn't feel comfortable with the sometimes tricky drying process. It took about eighteen mature roots (eighteen years or older) to make a pound. In twenty years' hunting he'd had three $1000 days. Out of work one fall, he supported his family "on the ginseng." He's since used it to supplement his income.

The state had recently become involved in the ginseng harvest. They'd set a picking season, from September 1 to November 30. The Department of Environmental Conservation oversees the licensing of exporters. The DEC's role is mandated by the United States Fish and Wildlife Service, which became involved after ginseng was classified an endangered species under the terms of CITES (Convention of the International Trade of Endangered Species) in the mid-'70s.

The kicker to many wild-ginsengers like Spanhake is the regulation which prohibits picking it on state land, where veteran hunters have planted it for generations. Spanhake rattled on about the DEC while we climbed a slope lumbered in the early '80s. He forged ahead, talking a blue streak, as I puffed behind, occasionally inserting a breathless question. When he spotted the kind of undergrowth and hardwood that ginseng like, we began bushwhacking uphill.

"The ginseng don't like fern," Spanhake said. "They like your hardwoods—maple, butternut, and ash. They like dry streambeds. They like it dry, but not too dry. They like shade, but not too much shade. You see nettles, you'll find ginseng. The ginseng like blue cohash, too."

Spanhake said that he used to hunt bobcat with a coon dog and that the Catskills (especially the area around Pine Hill) had the largest bobcat population in the state. I'd always dreamed of seeing a cat in the wild. After the snow fell, Spanhake said he'd bring me along to "call for cats," squeaking like a mouse by blowing against the back of his hand. I asked if it would be possible to breed bobcat with domestic cat. "Don't think so," he said. "One problem is domestic cat is one of bobcat's favorite foods. I've seen tracks coming right into the village."

He knew a place in West Virginia where he could get me a cub. He also told me about calls for turkey, fox, and coyote and said he'd been tempted to capture and raise a coyote pup that he'd been "pre-baiting" (a trapper's term) every morning on his way to work. "This high," he said, putting a flat hand against his knee. "I'd consider it, except for the children."

We were both bent low, ducking under branches, pushing uphill. "There's one," Spanhake said and bolted forward. The small plant was about fifteen feet away, hidden in the undergrowth, but somehow Spanhake had spotted it. I plopped down and examined the specimen. About a foot high, it grew in a slight hollow. Bright green leaves cradled a red berry nub. I'd seen the plant before. Spanhake knelt and coaxed the berries from their clasps. He crushed the red skin enfolding two small seeds the color and consistency of bone. I took a berry in my mouth; the familiar medicinal flavor of ginseng washed over my tongue, cheeks, and gums.

I asked Spanhake about ginseng's beneficial properties, which in oriental pharmacopoeia traditionally include longevity, regulation of imbalances in the circulatory system, and increased potency. He shrugged. "Been eating it for years. Don't think it's done anything for me."

Nevertheless, while carefully extracting the root, he sucked a mouthful of ginseng seeds. From marks that indicated where the yearly stem broke from the core, he determined the plant was about eighteen years old. Numerous hairs sprouted from the root, and he was careful not to damage them—hair pattern and root shape can send value soaring. Last year a man-shaped root sold in Taiwan for $21,000.

I munched on the white fibrous stalk while Spanhake replanted the seeds nearby. Replanting was instilled in him by his father and uncles. To them, ginseng was a lifelong pursuit, a way to live off the land.

Resuming our climb, we soon came to a northeast slope cloaked in nettles. We slogged through the brush in a zigzag pattern and halted after five minutes to take a harpooner's view from one of the large stones that dotted the terrain like sleeping whales. Spanhake said that the nettles might be camouflaging our prey; unless, of course, the ginseng had failed to come up this year (not likely) or someone had already raided this patch (a distinct possibility).

Greedy hunters can pick ginseng before it matures. If it's picked too early, the seeds don't have a chance to fall to the ground or be spread by foraging animals. On first frost the nettles wither; then ginseng leaves turn gold. That's prime picking; in fact, Spanhake declared, today was really just a scouting mission.

Suddenly all that changed.

"Found one!" he growled. "See if you can spot it."

All I saw were nettles and the broken ground.

Spanhake took four giant steps and knelt before a three-pronged plant, berries bobbing. We found four others in quick succession. Spanhake hadn't hunted there in six years, and the picking was good. He diligently sowed dozens of seeds.

We skirted the mountainside, heading up the notch, deeper and deeper into the woods. I asked Spanhake why he had stopped guiding. He said that it was too dangerous—his last client had discharged a .30-caliber rifle a dozen feet behind him. The bullet had whizzed past his ear and blasted a hole in a nearby tree. Wood chunks had slammed into Spanhake's chest, knocking him down.

"I thought I'd been hit. I just lay there, all the wind knocked out of me. Stunned. In shock. I couldn't move."

I asked Spanhake to explain the joys of turkey hunting (his prime passion). I'd always pictured it as a cold and dismal sport—you sit stone-still in one spot hours on end (usually in rain, sleet, or snow) coaxing a bird out of the woods who can see twenty times better than you.

Spanhake first assured me that wild turkey tastes good. All dark tender meat; his wife roasted them to perfection. Then he explained his devotion to the sport.

"The tables are turned. You're the hunted. The prey is the hunter."

It was like a seduction—a gentle, patient enticement.

Boasting in a matter-of-fact manner, he described his luring technique: "I've mastered all your gobbles, clucks, putts, yelps, and kikis." I asked for a demonstration, but he demurred.

He also sketched the world of competitive turkey shooters: those select few who, for example, have killed a bird in almost every state—the appeal of different venues where shooters congregate. The whole endeavor still sounded a bit goofy to me. No way you'd get me out there gobbling on a raw November morning.

We had kept to an old logging road, but began bush-whacking again, traversing a particularly steep and tricky scree of snarls and brambles. Spanhake momentarily lost his footing and had to right himself with his hand. The mountain dropped precipitously on our left. "One wrong step and you could take quite a tumble," he said.

We talked about Czajka. Spanhake had started him hunting ginseng. The two were once good friends, but they'd had a falling out. Spanhake said Czajka was a "ginseng hog"—a raider in the patches who picked everything in sight. I told him Czajka had hurt his ankle and wouldn't be going into the mountains this year.

"He's always got some excuse when someone wants to go with him." I remembered Czajka limping up the bank at Broadstreet Hollow. What a cagey old coot! "He's a game hog too," Spanhake said for good measure. "But boy! he knows how to fish. Not many guys on the Esopus, maybe four or five, who can pull them in like we do."

Grunting, Spanhake stooped and picked up a broken ginseng stem lying next to a fresh boot track. "Someone's been here before us. This morning." We cut downhill on no particular path. In five minutes we came to another torn stem. We were both amazed we were shadowing the hunter's trail. I hadn't realized how far back into the notch we'd walked. It took thirty minutes to get back to the car.

The morning with Spanhake fired me up. That evening over dinner I rhapsodized about ginseng to Erika and Sebastian Degens, my sister and brother-in-law visiting from Portland, Oregon. I announced that the next morning I would hike into the high country (following trails known only to myself) and find a mother lode of the valuable and reclusive plant. Sebastian agreed to accompany me and help carry down the bushels of ginseng we were sure to find.

Even with a late start we were in fine spirits as we began the hunt. No sooner had we entered the forest than Sebastian, an avid mycologist, pounced on an *Edulus boletus*, which the Italians call *porcini*. The *boletus* was a fine little mushroom with a calfskin top. Pleased, Sebastian plucked it from the ground and popped it into his special specimen bag.

We began the climb on a logging road through an area lumbered in the '70s. Even though I'd walked this way before, I took a wrong turn where the road forked. We began bushwhacking upslope but not before spotting a clump of *Armilaria mellia* (honey mushrooms). Sebastian, who holds duel American and German citizenship, said that the *Armilaria* are one of the few mushrooms which Europeans still consider safe to eat. Since Chernobyl, most continental mushrooms have had high concentrations of metals and radioactivity. The honey mushroom, however, got its protein from organic matter fixed in trees fifteen or twenty years ago.

I peeled my eyes as we climbed, but, though Sebastian found more mushrooms, I failed to find ginseng. We stalked through a high rocky area of mature hardwoods and nettles, an exact replica of the terrain Spanhake and I had combed the day before. Sebastian cut a funny figure, galumphing through the stingers, swatting them with a short stick he had procured from the forest floor for just this purpose, his forehead furrowed, his brow tense.

Watching him thrash about entertained me somewhat, but eventually, after we'd searched and searched and found nothing, I grew morose.

We broke for lunch on a high ridge with a long view west. Sebastian, to boost my spirits, regaled me with stories of the *Amanita muscaria*, thought by some mycologists to be the basis for the myth of Santa Claus: Red-and-white–capped, the European variety of the *muscaria* is hallucinogenic. Lapp reindeer would eat them. Then the Lapp would drink the reindeer urine. The active ingredients of the *muscaria*, extracted and purified, passed through the deer's digestive tracts. Sly beasts all! Rudolf! Prancer! Dasher! Dancer! Vixen! Blitzen! Cupid! Comet! Donder! Up, up and away!

Sebastian mentioned that a similar process occurs in Mexico, where dogs remove cyanide from peyote. We marveled at tribal man's elaborate practical knowledge of nature. Drinking reindeer urine—how positively ingenious! We wondered how scientific method had been reconciled with systems of magic and superstition based, it seemed to us, wholly on faith. The paradox somehow seemed germane to our quest. As wind wafted through the treetops, I reclined on a flat stone which warmed my back. Visions of sugarplums danced in my head, and I felt like dozing. I thought of Mary Oliver's superb poem, "Mushrooms":

> ...those who know
> walk out to gather, choosing
> the benign from flocks
> of glitterers, sorcerers,
> russulas,
> panther caps,
> shark-white death angels
> in their torn veils
> looking innocent as sugar

but full of paralysis:
to eat
is to stagger down
fast as mushrooms themselves
when they are done being perfect...

While discussing preference for food as a basic cultural trait, Sebastian said "Americans distrust mushrooms" (with an old-world chauvinism he sometimes assumes). I introduced the subject of poison mushrooms, a subject every true mycologist loves to address.

There had been a recent mushroom poisoning in Woodstock involving mistaken *chanterelles.* "Dumb, dumb, dumb, dumb, *dumb!*" said Sebastian when he heard. Two people had become very sick with symptoms including numbness and dizziness. Many mushroom poisons paralyze (as Oliver says); suffocation occurs when the breathing apparatus freezes. Basking drowsily on my warm stone I wondered what being poisoned would feel like. I imagined my chest cavity cold and numb, eyes fixed and glazed, jaw set, vertebrae stiffened. On the other hand, maybe paralysis would feel like complete relaxation—the body possessed by a force greater than itself, a surrendering, tongue touched by the sorcerer's wand, and then an ethereal suspension.

Sebastian said another *Aminita*, the *phallodes*, is also renowned and popularly known as the "death cap." Sebastian described its bulbous bottom, long stem, and pale-green cap (would you eat a pale-green mushroom?). On the West Coast it's typically found under wild chestnut trees.

He said that recently four people foraging for wild chestnuts in Portland came across a patch of *phallodes* (which they thought were straw mushrooms) and gobbled them down that night in a stir-fry. One of the most devious things about the death cap is that initially you're racked with spasms of nausea and diarrhea; but if you decide to "weather it out" (as mycologists like to say) you become suddenly better. Everything seems ginger-peachy until a week or two later when you experience renal failure. Two of the four needed liver transplants. The death cap yields a death rate of fifty percent.

Sebastian said there are thousands of mushrooms whose properties remain unknown. "That's one of the appeals of mycology. You can be an amateur and still make science." The adventurous nibble unknown specimens to test their effects. Sebastian intoned a myco-logical ditty: "There are old mushroomers, and there are bold mushroomers, but there are no old bold mush-roomers."

Gathering ourselves, we gradually descended a moun-tainside of nettles and blue cohash. We swatted, grunted, stumbled, thrashed, and poked. It was late afternoon by the time we found the water table and sat munching apples high on the headwaters of a tumbling stream. Brook trout darted in the pool at my feet. An hour's walk downstream, and we returned to roads, houses, and the anticipation of dinner, a hot shower, and family. We were tired and happy, but without any ginseng.

Talking about ginseng around town, the name Arthur Rashap kept coming up. Rashap was reputed to be the Catskill ginseng king. He was living in an enormous house in Roxbury and managing what was formally Margaret-ville's Cass Inn and is now Hanah Country Resort, owned by two Tokyo-based companies: Koizumi Company Lim-ited and Taisei Honsho.

In the '70s, Rashap, a lawyer, moved from New York City to Woodstock, where he lived briefly before going west to Delaware County. His involvement with ginseng has been intensive and longlasting. He founded the first

U.S. Ginseng Institute, originally located in Philadelphia, then Roxbury, and now Wawsaw, Wisconsin.

Rashap buys and sells wild ginseng and operates two ginseng farms, in Hobart and Catskill. Initially, the farms had been a source of great hope; now they've become a source of *tsuris*. Bearded chin in hand, puppy dog eyes wistful but not without humor, Rashap says at one time he had hoped that cultivated Catskill ginseng would provide "right livelihood" and make him rich beyond his wildest dreams. Instead, it has strained him, both financially and personally: Wildlife prey upon plants devastated by insects and disease; the soil has become highly acidic; his crops are feeble and stunted; poachers help themselves. "Karma?" he asks, gazing heavenward.

Rashap has led a complex life. As we talk, his point of reference shifts from lawyer to foundation director, non-profit "maven" to ginseng fiend, golf fanatic to gourmand, frustrated writer to corporate consultant. Many things, he's a mite scattered and very appealing.

Rashap feeds me leftover Chinese food (a true New Yorker, he apologized several times for its marginal quality) and attempts to explain *The Doctrine of Signatures* (which has something to do with ingestion, internal balance, and the seasons). In walks Rick Clark, who'd dug a pound of fresh ginseng over the weekend with his girlfriend and wants to unload it. I follow Rashap and Clark into the dining room where a dealer's scale sits on a large table. They weigh the goods while I shoot the buy.

Clark departs. Rashap spins out ginseng miscellany. The root was the colonies' largest export (30,000 to 50,000 pounds yearly, he estimates) and both George Washington (as a surveyor) and Daniel Boone were heavily into the stuff. John Jacob Astor made his first money in the ginseng trade. Today the U.S. exports 220,000 pounds annually—50,000 to 70,000 pounds wild—much of the rest supplied by 1,500 ginseng farmers in Marathon

County, Wisconsin. Marathon's yearly crop grosses fifty to ninety million dollars. The Catskill end of total U.S. business is small—1,000 to 1,500 pounds—although we account for thirty to fifty percent of New York State's yield. Tennessee, West Virginia, and Kentucky each produce approximately 10,000 pounds wild a year.

I follow Rashap upstairs to a garret filled with books and articles—all on ginseng. One of the Institute's first projects was an indexed bibliography, which Rashap hands over. It's full of entries like the following: Anisimov, M. M., Prokofieva, N. G., Kusnetsova, T. A., and Pertotolchin, N. V. 1971: The effect of some triterpene glycosides on protein synthesis in tissue culture of the bone marrow of rats. Izv. Akad Nauk SSSR Ser., I:137–40. Russian. Not exactly a layman's guide. I ask for something more accessible.

A muttering Rashap plunges through boxes for more material. Finally, he gives me *The Tao of Medicine* by Stephen Fulder. I scan Fulder on ginseng as aphrodisiac: "fresh ginseng with soya, ox-penis and dried human placenta...the tongues of a hundred peacocks, spiced with chilies and the sperm of pubescent boys." Then Fulder mentions that Arab potentates bought $250,000 worth of ginseng the previous year.

We head downstairs, and Rashap proudly shows off his ginseng collection. Everywhere I turn there's ginseng. Roots are framed and mounted on the walls. A large multicolored portrait of a ginseng root by a Woodstock artist I don't know hangs in the dining room. Rashap exudes a faint incredulity over this gap in my knowledge. He pauses as though deciding whether to hold it against me or if it impairs whatever it is we've got going. Neither is the case. We enter a small studio where he paints watercolors of Chinese landscapes. Rashap unscrews a Mason jar packed with ginseng roots marinating in vodka and offers me a swig. It is surprisingly smooth. I read later that spiking vodka with ginseng is an old Soviet trick said by some to induce a pristine drunk, free from hangover.

In fact, the Soviets are big on ginseng. The root has spawned a folk culture replete with mystical tales; many are medieval and suggest an obsession with faith. As the Elder Zossima's eyes are to Alyosha, so ginseng is to wandering seers who live off air and pursue rumors of the plant deep into the wilderness of central Asia. These hunters are a crazed lot, dressed in tatters, raving, lunatic, but supremely beautiful and blessed in their devotion. More recently, Soviet athletes have used ginseng like steroids, to manufacture muscle and boost performance. I ask Rashap's fourteen-year-old son Raven if he consumes the plant which has consumed his father. "Sometimes," he says. "Before soccer games."

I leave Rashap's, arms piled with books and ginseng samplers. Driving toward Margaretville, I run into an early fall hatch so thick that I have to stop and use a rag to wipe the insects off the windshield.

I'm back at Rashap's a week or so later to pick up a couple pounds of fresh ginseng which I was planning to sell in the city. During the interim, I've read *The Tao of Medicine*, a provocative analysis of Eastern versus Western medicine and pharmacology. (My favorite gleaning from Fulder: In traditional Chinese medicine doctors were paid to keep you healthy and were fined if you got sick.)

The ginseng king is not around, but there's a note attached to the stash. He needs to get at least $75 a pound, and I should refrigerate when not using. I unseal one of the plastic bags and take a deep whiff of fresh ginseng aroma, astringent and earthy. The next day I call Rashap to get the names and addresses of two exporters.

The following day I find myself heading east on Canal Street toting two pounds of Catskill root to sell in Chinatown, the last leg of my ginseng journey. My first stop is John Louie on Lafayette Street. Rashap had told me that Louie's family had been exporting ginseng for four generations.

I ascend the stairs and enter a hall redolent with a scent now familiar to me. Louie is away, but a young female assistant, who identifies herself only as Mary, and Louie's father, Har Fook Louie, are holding down the fort. The office is modern and antiseptic, not at all the exotic caravansary I'd been expecting. Mary and Har Fook inspect my ginseng. Although intrigued, they suggest that I return when the root has dried; it's no use to them fresh. I ask how they gauge wild Catskill ginseng. Mary consults Har Fook in Chinese. Quite good, she reports; perhaps not the very best, but right up there.

The elder Louie is elegant, gentle, and almost heartbreakingly polite. He's 5'7" and not more than 115 pounds. He has white hair brushed back off his forehead, a blue suit that articulates his lithe body, and perfectly relaxed posture. I ask him about the difference between wild and cultivated ginseng and how the world ginseng market flows. Mary interprets.

All the root he gathers is shipped to Hong Kong where it is sorted for size and shape then distributed throughout Asia. Har Fook disparages ginseng from Appalachia; he prefers the northern strains. We compare color and weigh in our palms the density of my wild Catskill compared to cultivated Wisconsin. My stuff is heavier and darker.

"Now you know all!" says Mary as I exit.

Not quite! But I do feel some of the elder Louie's gentle manner has rubbed off on me as I continue toward the Bowery, where I direct my steps to a restaurant on East Broadway extolled by a friend for its hacked eel. The roast ducks and chickens dangling in the window look foul indeed. I nourish myself instead on familiar *dim sum* at the restaurant HSF. Several plates of steamed shrimp dumplings inside me, I lean back, drink tea, and survey the scene: the extended Chinese family gatherings; the white crowd feeding exotics to their out-of-town friends. Slipping into the alleys of Bayard and Pell Streets, I proclaim "wild Catskill ginseng!" to shopkeepers rooting through my bag. Like Louie, they're not interested in the fresh root. They want dry.

Then at one apothecary, I get my first offer—$75 for both pounds. I look suitably aggrieved and hit the street. Maybe I've had enough of Chinatown. Aside from Louie, the other address Rashap had slipped me is in the garment district. I make for the subway but get caught up in the mercantile spirit when back on Canal Street. I pop into Ten Ren Tea and Ginseng Co., Inc., a spiffy shop that sells only ginseng and tea. Counter girls in their twenties are all dressed in the same green-and-white uniforms. One runs to fetch the manager when I expose my wares.

"North New York!" says Mark M. Lii, appreciatively sniffing. He's a big man, my age, with a shock of black hair and lightly tinted glasses with heavy frames. He beckons me to a glossy wood table surrounded by a set of matching chairs carved in an intricate crane motif. I face a photo of George Bush sipping tea with Lii. (Why not munching on ginseng? I wondered.) Lii disappears to weigh the goods. He returns and offers me $75 a pound. "Done!" I say, and he counts the bills into my hand.

I exit Ten Ren thirty minutes later after a most convivial chat, buoyed by the deal just cut. A dwarf plays dominos on the bottom of a cardboard box. The street smells of urine and duck fat. My ginseng is on its way to Hong Kong, then to Jakarta, Kobe, Shanghai, Mandalay, or some other exotic destination, to be consumed by someone who probably has never even imagined the Catskills. I wish them well, a long and healthy life, a thousand cranes.

It's dusk by the time I cross the George Washington Bridge and head north on the Palisades Parkway. Cracking the window, I feel a cool sliver of night whip across my face like an invisible flag. Soon I'm exiting north onto the Thruway, spinning the car in a tight torque, the traffic light.

The artery of the Thruway is my original directional, the arrow on my internal compass. In Negril, Sinai, or Tokyo I can close my eyes and see it running north–south. It's embedded in my mind's map, inscribed early. Of the hundreds of times I've traveled this route, most were as a child. We spent weekends in the country until my father (then a Wall Street lawyer) said "FUCK IT" and moved us to Woodstock for good.

North of Harriman I have the road to myself. Star Mountain is there and Storm King and the endless miles of orchards heavy with fruit. It's colder now and I roll up the window. I'm in my baffled cocoon, a tiny speck of consciousness flickering. The engine purrs, and I feel immense gratitude to my father who had the courage to desert the glitz and money of New York City and adopt something simpler and saner. I hear his voice deep inside me. I see with his eyes and speak with his tongue. Once in a while a light gleams on the quiet hills.

LIVING OFF
THE LAND

IT HAD BEEN seventeen years since I last shook Bob Cross's hand. "How you been keeping?" he asked. Cross folded my hand with his own and smiled in his pleased way. Marguerite, his wife, hurried from the kitchen and kissed me on the cheek. Snow hissed outside the living room's picture window on Cold Brook Road. From this vantage, Cross could gaze across the Wittenberg Valley to Wittenberg Estates, a subdivision he'd recently laid out for Victor Zeines, a local dentist and developer.

After we had settled in and chatted about family, the conversation turned, as always, to land. "Some people have told me they can't stand that house up there," said Marguerite, referring to a large new house in the Zeines development poised on the mountainside like a loud unthinking noise. "But I've gone up there and stood on the deck, and what a view! Let me tell you *it is something*! If I could afford it I'd move up there myself."

In seventeen years she had broadened and grayed, as had her husband; but like their house, she'd remained

19

much the same. She glided about with a stately drift, elbows floating at her sides. The serene matriarchal air had deepened in her full-moon face and high cheekbones.

Cross, on the other hand, had slowed. There was a stiffness in his joints, a frailty. Not surprising for a man of sixty, but incongruous with my memory of him—a man of deliberate fluidity and concentrated strength. He had kept the beard, now white, which I remembered so well. Though his private self remained enigmatic as always, his reserve had lifted—the warmth and disappointments closer to the surface.

I'd contacted Cross because I'd always been curious about surveyors. I wanted to understand their knowledge of terrain and be able to look at the landscape through their eyes. I'd wintered in the house of a surveyor in Anchorage, Alaska, and my memory of him preyed on me. He was given to fits of brutality, alternating with spells of sweetness. He worked the Prudhoe Bay oil fields— twelve-hour days, seven-day weeks, six weeks at a time. Then four weeks off, and he'd come home and debauch through the strip joints and coke dens of that boom-bust town. He was well paid, but he exuded a feral scent, as though his expertise and education were just a facade.

Like the few surveyors I've known before and since, he occupied an odd position in society—a professional without prestige; an essentially physical man doing head work; a blue-collar laborer with a white-collar paycheck. The garage in Anchorage was full of gear: a drafting table, intricate rulers, stakes and ribbons, all-weather snow suits (good to 50^0 below), moon boots with plastic casings, and lantern helmets with which he braved the 24-hour arctic night. That winter he sited huge platforms on the tundra (for what horrible purpose I can't recall). As he described his calculations, I was amazed at their delicacy. And I wondered—is he miner or architect? Carpenter or engineer? Drone or guide?

Reacquainting myself with Cross, these questions, though not completely irrelevant, weren't pressing. Cross was hooked into the country end of surveying, where the surveyor molds how the area comes to be the way it is. Sometimes he even knows why. Cross had run his own business for the past thirty years. Answerable to no one but himself, he had built a reputation for accurate, honest work. He'd been the prime mover in founding the Mid-Hudson Valley Association of Professional Surveyors and a director of the State Land Surveyors Association, as well as serving terms as its treasurer, vice president, and president. I'd always been drawn to Cross because of his pride in his profession and love for his work.

I had a personal interest in Cross, as well. A minor though important figure in my life, he'd helped to shape the values I now live by—the allegiance I feel to the outdoors and rural life. I needed to reestablish that connection, to look again at where I had been and where I was going, and assess the perspective he'd helped give me.

Dogs barked in the yard, muffled by snow. We were still on the Zeines project. Marguerite aimed her volubility in my direction: "Who are we to tell people where they can and can't live? What they can and can't do with their land? It's the 'close the door behind me' attitude. 'Now that I'm here I don't want anyone else allowed in!' "

"He knows! He knows!" Cross broke in, laughing.

And, indeed, I did know. Also visible from Cross's window, beyond the Zeines development, was the edge of Riverby Wittenberg, which Cross had surveyed and which had brought him into my life, briefly, long ago.

In the early '70s, my father, a lawyer, became a land developer and hired Cross to survey a large subdivision. Cross was one of a local crew who balanced my father's New York City investors. Although the investors espoused liberal causes and had a vaguely altruistic air, they were into money. Lawyers and businessmen, they were nonetheless in a rough lineage with my parents' earlier associates who paraded their ventures and causes through our doors and defined my world.

The earlier types had been mainly marginal: nudist communalists, orgone fanatics, conspiracy junkies, and anarchist pistoleros. My father's professionalism lent them a legit veneer. Riverby (which took its name from the home of the nineteenth-century local naturalist, poet, and philosopher John Burroughs) was a natural succession from the school with no rules which my father had helped found, the defunct lecture hall with which he had sought to free himself from practicing law, and the tacky camp he had tried to resuscitate. Riverby suited his brand of idealism. He called it an ecological development. The oxymoron drove locals mad. It was a 923-acre model of his personal escape. He had taken issue with the city. It was going downhill, it was deadly and debasing, it stank, it was violent. When Woodstock reacted to the influx of new people and the change they augured and said "Go away, we don't want you," my father was incensed. He stormed "How dare they refuse to extend a life line?"

What happened to Woodstock in the mid-'60s was Dylan's doing, of course, not my father's. Dylan redefined and broadened the élan attached to Woodstock's name. He unwittingly prompted the town's expansion and transformation. It's a fascinating progression: Dylan sleeping over the Espresso Cafe, the late-'60s "sound-ins" in Pam Copeland's field, the '69 festival, and the music mecca Woodstock became during the '70s in a scene which centered around The Joyous Lake.

Dylan and my father were drawn to Woodstock's character, a mix of bohemia and backwoods. They both used what people like Cross represented to construct fictions of hard winters, raw springs, exile and redemption, repudiation and homecoming. In Woodstock, Dylan shed the vestiges of his Greenwich Village ascension and concocted his own version of country. His 1966–68 exodus—which took him from the album cover of *Bringing It All Back Home* (pictured in the height of rural chic with a mod Sally Grossman) to the cover of *John Wesley Harding*, a woodsman flanked by Appalachia Nashville folk—now seems like a set-up, heralding the next leap into the parodical world of Johnny Cash and New Morning.

In the early '70s, when Riverby debuted, Dylan moved back to MacDougal Street, perhaps tiring of Woodstock's new image which he had helped spawn. My father took flak from all sides—too capable for a town which prided itself on being a refuge for inspired amateurs and occasionally intriguing failures. Cross and some of the other locals (those with whom he did business) stood by him. I reciprocated. It was in those years prior to college that I took to the mountains, and this only strengthened the respect I felt for people like Cross, who'd hunted, fished, trapped, logged, quarried, and farmed the land for generations.

In Riverby's early days, my father did business from a tepee and let hippies live in the hemlock forest near the mountaintop. They pitched tepees of their own and erected torii and shrines. One summer night we visited their fire circle, the singe of cannabis trickled through the shadows. Michael Green, an eternally ephebic type in a white robe, explained that he now uses grass rarely; when he did, it was to reprogram his life and change things in himself that needed changing. A doeish woman diddled a wood flute. I wanted them to stay forever.

If Riverby's money-men saw themselves as progenitors, shaping the world in which they lived, the local crew, perhaps less grandiose, were no less motivated. They were a physical bunch in boots and plaid shirts who liked to work and accommodated themselves to the Riverby style.

In my mind, Cross will always be linked to Jimmy Cousins, who built Riverby's roads. Cousins was a rambunctious man who died in a helicopter crash before he turned forty. He played in the weekly $.75-limit poker game often held at our house, which I used to watch. The game was dealer's choice, and Cousins always dealt five-card stud. No matter what card he had showing, he raised when the bet came around. A steady winner, he seemed naturally lucky. He gleamed behind his stacks of change; exuberance, barely checked, flashed in his tight smile.

In his contracting work, Cousins cut wide swaths through the landscape, while Cross worked almost in code. Small ribbons fluttering on trees were Cross's spoor, the calculated whispers of his passage. The bounds he delineated went unnoticed. Like Cousins, Cross's demeanor reflected his work. He was quiet and unobtrusive, his interior, like his bounds, shown by modest indicators placed few and far between.

Cousins's death left a void which brought my family and the Crosses together. Cross taught me how to use a chain saw—legs apart, balance set, never work above the waist, never uppercut, watch the knots, don't hurry. In the summer of 1974, our two families planted a communal vegetable garden in a field long fallow, near a luxurious house my parents had built on the come of Riverby's anticipated spoils.

For the building site, my father had five acres clear cut. The house had dozens of picture windows and custom tile work and was floored with deep-gray carpet. In many ways, it was prototypical of the homes built here since. Walking over the carpet, static collected in your body like a cyclotron, to be discharged by a touch that felt as though you had stuck a fork deep into an operating toaster.

We turned over a 100 x 100–foot plot for the garden. The furrows smelled of pumpernickel. Clearing the ground of larger stone, I remember we stranded one gray monster that didn't seem worth the bother. The carryable ones we cupped in our arms, and the back-breakers we rolled out end over end. Big stuff vanquished, our fingers sifted the earth to pull out the small stuff. Soon fingers and palms were talced with dirt; I wondered that it didn't moisten our skin but dried it instead. Swooping, I chucked a parade of stones into the blue. I can still feel their heft in my hand; trace the afterimage of an arced right arm; hear them whomp into the woods, ricochets ringing, the horizon like spilt milk. No matter how many stones we pulled, more remained. They rose up under our hands.

Before sowing, we built an eight-foot fence against the deer. Cross dispatched his eldest boy Bobby and me to cut cedar posts. That cedar was tough. I thought it'd break the chain saws, whirring super-hot through trunks that were coiled like cables. The posts were so hard, they hurt to handle. Dropped, they bounced unbending. Knocked, they rang like rails. "*Damn* this cedar," we said, firing up the saws in the black fly-clotted humid afternoon. What makes it so damn hard?

Long rows were planted. I'll always remember the morning when I walked to the garden to find seedlings had appeared. It was miraculous. Cross shared my excitement. Though he'd been raised on a farm in North Lexington, and his family had been farmers for generations, he found each germination infinitely sweet.

Deer tracked the ground around the fence as our plants grew. It was as if they hungered for only what we'd sown. It was clear from the tracks that they'd stood gazing inward toward our crop, stomping in frustration. In my dreams, I felt their velvet muzzles twitch deep within my palm. The deer were successfully repelled, but a woodchuck managed to infiltrate the wire. We let him stay in his elaborate burrow under the zucchini—not that we could have ousted him had we tried. Cross reminisced about the woodchuck, saying "Those buggers can get in a garden and raise heck with you. They especially like peas and beans. Level 'em right to the ground." Asked why we'd made the garden so big, he replied, "Well, it's like most things. You always start out with grandiose plans."

Seventeen years after the garden, after our luxurious house had been sold and the last of Riverby Wittenberg's lots finally bought, I bushwhacked uphill in a blizzard. Cross trudged before me, out on one of his rare field days with the crew. He carried a hatchet. His nephew, Jim Goodrich, who was in his early thirties and up ahead, lugged a range pole in addition to the standard-issue machete strapped to his side.

Robert Morris and Bill Degraw, both in their twenties, were out of sight, absorbed by the forest of maple and beech. They packed the heavy equipment—the Top Con Total Station and Tripod which measures distance and angle. Cross was in the early stages of a perimeter survey of the 375-acre Winlow Farm, which straddles the townships of Roxbury, Middletown, and Bovina.

This was my second field expedition with Cross's crew. I'd first become acquainted with Jim and Bill on what was supposed to be a quick jaunt to Ski Windham but turned out to consume the better part of a day. "So you're going to write the complete history of Robert G. Cross," said Bill to me that day, as he recorded distances from the Total Station's computerized read-out.

Japanese made, the station retails for about $14,000. It sends a beam of light to the center of a prism mounted on a range pole. Jim placed the pole at strategic points, outlining the culverts, buildings, and roads around the Wintergreen Club, a posh slope-side backgammon and drinking hangout. The beam bounced back to the station, which recorded its travel time then instantly computed the distance between the two points.

I playfully hassled Bill—a big man, fair-skinned, broad-shouldered, and puppyish—who seemed to invite minor persecutions. He'd been graduated from Cross's alma mater, the College of Forestry at Syracuse University. Like many before him, Bill was drawn to surveying because it's outdoor work. As we chatted in the early spring sunshine, however, he said he had doubts about his fledgling career: There were the freezing days of the December before last, the coldest on record, when Cross sent Bill miles up steep mountainsides carrying seventy pounds of gear. "Don't think I didn't question myself about surveying. Don't think I didn't have big questions," he said, squinting through the station telescope and nodding sagaciously, the voice of experience.

Then there was the last outfit he worked for, which recorded points in code. A tree was not a tree but a "3-22-8." The same was true for fences, culverts, and every other little thing, and Bill was always bawled out when he botched the notations.

Later that day Bill was quietly but firmly bossed by Jim. Perhaps the dynamic began as I watched Bill scrap with a small knoll on the way to fetch the car; he turned the slight rise into a grand obstacle, flourishing his machete at a few mangy brambles. "What's he doing?" I asked Jim. Jim smiled without meeting my eye and shook his head.

Cross and crew laid out much of the surveying for Ski Windham, Inc. They ran aerial topos from Hensenville clear through to Ashland, plotted chairlift paths and pilings, and mapped a subdivision that's now filling up with $500,000 homes. Quarter-acre building lots sell for $125,000–$150,000. Each lot comes with a ski easement, providing front-door access to the slopes.

I followed stick figures paralleling on the cant as Bill

bellowed "Yup" each time his beam struck the prism. He entered shots in a black log book.

Surveying work was once done with a sixty-six foot chain broken into a hundred parts. Measurements have grown increasingly exact, off by only one foot per 30,000 —though it's common to be off only one in 100,000, according to Cross. The work's also become quicker, more expensive, and, I would venture to add, routine. Sitings take a matter of seconds.

Jim quickly covered the two-acre lot, placing the range pole where the spirit took him, outlining salient topographical features and "improvements." Bill's notes filled four full pages in his black book. The coordinates were to be entered into a computer, which plots them on a map.

I tried to imagine the ancient roots of the profession as Jim and Bill worked. In Egypt, Babylon, and Greece, astronomy and surveying were like Siamese twins—linked by cartographic techniques—the devices used to calculate angle, height, and the geometric measurement of distance and form. Looking at pre-history, I think it's possible that surveying is tied to the origins of writing, when storytellers sketched pictures of homes and fields in the dirt as visual aids. Over time these abstracted into pictograms, ideograms, and script.

The history of surveying has yet to be written. My cursory glance at the field reveals no East-West comparative work, although reference is made to the antiquity of surveying in China. Several sources argue that it predates Western origins, but the evidence is slight. The history of technology places surveying on the edge of the far larger field of engineering.

It's in Roman times that I found the first comprehensive account of the profession. The expanding empire involved laying out quite a few lot lines. Roman surveyors were called *Agrimensores*, or "measurers of land." They developed manuals, codified land law, were dispatched with expeditionary forces, sat on land commissions (like today's municipal planning boards), settled boundary disputes, drew maps, developed curricula, and organized themselves into a profession with privileges and a well-defined expertise. To me, more compelling than the technical accomplishments of the field was that phase in the development of the profession when surveyors were storytellers—holy men who kept a record of the tribe and 3,000 years ago placed votive stones in farmers' fields, endowing them with taboos ("woe shall befall him that enters here"). The coordination of time and space, the conceptualization of nature (extracting what's perceived of as its skeleton, its geometry) was originally a mystical act that exploded mortality and our earthbound limits, as Stonehenge and the pyramids testify. These monuments were among surveyors' first accomplishments.

There's allure and adventure in the modern origins of the field. The profession flourished when Europe set sail in the fifteenth century, charting and claiming new lands that began at the shorelines. Men like Lincoln, Jefferson, and Washington were surveyors. Their work helped them think deeply on what this country was about, where it was going, and where they wanted it to go. Surveyors have traditionally been explorers and pioneers, blazing trails and opening territory.

Cross explained his attraction to surveying. "I would have liked to be a pioneer, experienced the unspoiled nature of the country. Seen it unchanged. I'd like to have lived when hunting was a way of life. When it wasn't questioned. I remember even as a child fifty years ago, there was a common bond between people. Very little selfishness. When a neighbor was sick you'd go over and do his chores. And he'd do the same for you. There was no talk of payment. Money wasn't so much a part of life."

Asked if he thinks it's ironic that he's helped destroy the very qualities of the country he loves, Cross heaved a sigh. He said he likes to think that he's helped mitigate the environmental damage, so often a result of development, and that the march of what people call progress is inexorable. "Though it does disturb me sometimes," he admitted. Cross lamented the current predicament of his profession, which has lost much of the prestige it traditionally enjoyed. Why? Cross said because surveyors are generally loners. Until recently they failed to establish professional organizations. They didn't keep pace as other related professions upped their educational requirements. Consequently, U.S. surveyors have watched the scope of the work they're legally entitled to do narrow. This is not the case in Europe and Canada.

"I'm the last of my breed," said Cross from his brick office in Shokan. "The last that'll be able to do subdivisions."

The governmental agencies which regulate land use and development require an engineer's signature on work once done by surveyors: sewage and road design, drainage and soil studies. Cross has fought hard against this trend in the professional organizations he's helped found.

Though Cross's office is located in Shokan it makes sense that he landed the Windham job. His roots are in Greene County. Four generations of Crosses farmed the North Lexington homestead. The family is Dutch-English and has resided in the area since the American Revolution, when a Cross served in the Lexington militia.

Cross's father died at forty-six of pancreatic cancer. Initially, Cross's mother rented out the 196-acre farm for $100 a month, equipment included; she sold out for $15,000 in 1958.

It hurts Cross to talk about the death of his father and the sale of their farm. Farming's in his blood. He talks wistfully of the days when he'll retire from surveying and move to his in-laws' farm in Lexington. "I'll miss being with the animals. I miss it. I really do." As he said this

I could feel it in him—the comfort, companionship, and peace. This was a man who could stay quiet for hours.

Windham's been good to Cross. But ten years of more or less steady work is nearing completion. The Catskills's real estate boom of the '80s has also played itself out. These days Cross has been hurting. His crew works every other week, drawing unemployment the rest of the time. The operation's pared to bare bones. Cross is concerned, though not panicky; he's been around too long for that.

It doesn't help that what little work Cross does have is often frustrated by the amount of time he spends dealing with regulatory agencies. He said that twenty years from now, holding and improvement costs on land will be so high that only the rich will be able to afford ownership. He said that the New York City Water Department has been grabbing the parts of the Catskills that remain in private hands. A new feudal order approaches!

We were driving from the office west to the Winlow Farm along Route 28 in Cross's posh touring van. "I always knew I was a hunter. It's a strong instinct," Cross said. Even though his dad had never stalked an animal before, Cross talked him into it when he was fourteen. His father shot a buck, a trophy head Cross has mounted in his living room. The next year his father was dead.

Cruising through Margaretville into the farmland of Middletown, Cross railed in his quiet way against animal rights groups. He spotted a wild turkey and gauged the fishing potential of a roadside brook. When we arrived at the farm, the crew was already donning gear. We started up the old farm road toward the forest where Bobby had left off the traverse the day before. (A traverse is an interior box from which the crew shoots outbounds. The line we were running that day was 4,400 feet and scooted over the mountaintop to God knows where.)

As we started out, the mid-morning sun was strong, reflecting off three inches of fresh snow. We had to squint against its glare, and walking was a chore. Our boots sank through the snow and slipped in the mud underneath. When Cross, winded, stopped two hundred yards in, my heart was racing.

"Sitting in the office all the time. It'll kill you," he said in disgust. Jim, panting, bemoaned the sedentary end of the job. Too much time spent in front of the computer. Bill and Robert dawdled at the meadow's edge as though they hadn't a care in the world. Clouds congealed in the sky so bright a moment before.

"Youth. It's a wonderful thing," said Cross, still breathing heavily. "I should get out in the field more. I really should."

We resumed the climb through flurries then squall. As we entered the woods, the slope steepened. We booted footholds, grabbed young tree trunks, and heaved ourselves uphill. The younger men were out of sight on the mountain's crest.

"If my doctor knew...I was doing this he'd scream and holler." Cross halted again and bent over, thigh clutched in both hands.

"What's wrong?"

"It's my heart. It's pounding—pounding in my ears."

Several vessels were clogged, and he was due in for more tests—which he'd put off. Admittedly, the exertion of the climb was risky, probably foolish. Nevertheless we continued.

"During hunting season I could motor up the mountain pretty good."

I should have sat down and refused to budge. Cross would have had to return to the car with me; after all, he was my host. But I did no such thing. I dogged his steps, snapping photos and scribbling notes (Cross on death: "It's got to be hard on everyone else. Once you're dead you're dead."). Was he serious?

Jim, who must have felt concern, didn't say anything

either. Let patriarchs dispose of themselves as they would; we were men with jobs to do! One of us might keel over in the snow and turn purple. No disgrace in dying with those bloody boots on.

By the time we arrived at the edge of the wide summit where work had stopped the day before, Bill had set up and manned his station. Jim—off on a tangent—described a corner, scoping it out. Range pole touching ground like a divining rod, he shot blazes, big trees, cairns, and a fence. Robert hacked brush, his machete dancing, and partially cleared a grown-over traverse cut by the last survery in 1972.

It was a complex job. The eastern border of the property lies on one of the old Hardenburgh Great Lot lines and is also the town line between Roxbury and Bovina. So it's apt to be well marked. Several property disputes on other lines have gone to court and are still contested. Cross would take the field data his crew gathered, compare deeds from the Delaware County Clerk's office in Delhi, weigh contradictory evidence, and whittle down the margin for error. The final map to which he'd affix his name is a legal document; though charged with impartiality, his fee is paid by a vested interest.

Leaving the crew behind, we forged ahead. On level ground, Cross hit his stride and chugged along. Flitting around the '72 crew's work, he offered a running critique. He sleuthed for signs of an older line, gouging a corner off a blaze with the hatchet that he'd carried from the car. Eighteen rings—clearly the '72 crew's work.

We entered a recently lumbered plateau and clambered over downed trees. I felt as though I was walking in the wake of a giant who's threaded over the mountaintop, ripping up the arbor like asparagus, biting off bottoms and tossing the tops to rot. Cross said it looked like a typical operation—logging's a messy business. We weren't turning up anything except possible hanky-panky. Perhaps the loggers, hired by a neighbor, had cut into our lot. The practice is not uncommon and is particularly irksome to Cross. Loggers often try to justify their trespass by forging survey blazes.

The crew caught up to us. They were none too pleased that their line plunged deep into a valley just discernible through the driving snow. The afternoon's work would be affliction and misery, and I was relieved when Cross said he had no intention of continuing.

Slugging water from a seltzer bottle I'd packed, I hitched my foot to a stump. "Your foot's right on line," drawled Jim with a hint of acerbity, the first I'd heard in his voice. It reminded me of Cross.

He pointed to Bill peering through the station's tele-scope, a hundred feet back. I removed my foot sheepishly, feeling like a quitter for sticking with them only half a day. At noon sharp the crew knocked off for lunch. Even in front of the man they work for they were taciturn, almost testy.

Following the traverse down the mountain back to the car, we detoured to inspect a corner, which involved lurching across several hundred yards of steep, slippery ground. Once off the mountain, the squall abated. Cross was peeved that he was wearing his flat-soled boots and said he felt sorry for Bill. The station's telescope magnified snowflakes; they appeared as meteors, hurtling into the viewfinder. Bill the long-suffering! He broke into a tough profession. I couldn't understand why it was taking so long to find the damn corner! Cross snooped, poked, and circled then finally found it.

I wanted to get off that mountain. When we headed out, I set the pace, nearly skipping, schussing through powder coating into dead leaves. Out of the woods, Cross resumed the lead. Snow pelted the meadows, but nothing like what the crew was experiencing on the mountain-top. Nearing the van, Cross slipped and buckled, going down hard, and smashing his knee. "I'll feel that tomorrow!"

He struggled to his feet, slapped mud from his pants, and flexed the joint. The first wave of pain took a minute to subside. We lost track of the crew on the walkie-talkie once we were back at the car. They'd started down the mountain's backside.

In Margaretville we dropped in on fellow surveyor Robert Allison, who was out in the field, lunched at the Bun and Cone, and inspected the local hardware store's enormous collection of trophy-size buck heads.

"Look at that," sighed Cross. "Sixty heads, all trophy. It's unreal."

"Bob Cross in heaven," I said, snapping his photo. He chuckled.

On the drive home we talked of hunting, fishing, farming, and the vicissitudes of real estate development. Cross said he'd been tempted several times but had seen too many deals turn sour. He pointed up the mountain in Fleischmann's. Several years before, a developer he was working for made a honey of a deal. He bought the whole mountain, a huge chunk of land *with* houses, for only a pittance and stood to make millions. Then the market collapsed. The developer was over-committed, pushing in too many directions. He couldn't meet his holding costs and sold out to partners for a fair piece of change, but nothing near like what he'd stood to profit.

"It's like a bug that gets them," said Cross. "They can't just stick to one thing."

I knew what he was talking about. The same thing happened to Riverby soon after the vegetable garden had been planted. Riverby became the largest land developer in the country. Its holdings totaled thousands of acres. Then the recession hit, and oil prices shot up. My father refused bankruptcy; it took ten years for him to free himself of debt.

Cross dropped me off. I told him that he should go in for those tests, that there were new methods for dealing with clogged arteries. We talked briefly about my father's two bouts with open-heart surgery. The first was when the economy collapsed in the mid-'70s and left him holding the bag. The second was thirteen years later, the previous fall. Cross listened carefully and nodded. I thanked him for the day, and we shook hands.

I'd come to say goodbye. I drove up Erika's Walk in Riverby Wittenberg, which Cousins had built and my father named after my sister. Most of the lots Cross surveyed now hold houses, invisible through the trees in full leaf. A deed restriction requires homes to be out of sight of the road.

I own fifteen acres of Riverby land with my sister. We'd decided to sell and had a buyer. As the closing approached I'd put off taking a last look. "It must be kind of sad for you," said Cross when I told him we were in contract. On the way to the land a sporty white car driven by a young man in aviator shades and a white baseball cap overtook me and began to tailgate. I felt like shoving his face in the 35 mph signs posted along the roadside. I realized how angry I felt and pulled over to let him pass. He stepped on it and was gone in a flash.

Our land was at the head of Erika's Walk. I parked by an old logging road cut by Nelson Shultis when he'd lumbered there before selling to Riverby. Packing a couple of extra shirts, kitchen matches, and a pad, I headed into the hemlock forest at the eastern end of the property. The light was murky under the hemlocks, then the forest changed to hardwood and laurel. I could see the summits of the big peaks in the southern Catskills and the western sky which was just beginning to color at its fringe. The evening was cool and crisp.

I tarried at the place where I used to imagine that I'd build a house, when I lived far away and was feeling particularly dejected. Minor clearing and it would command a sweeping view. There, at the house site, the woods were a mix of mountain laurel and white birch.

The birch caught the redness deepening in the west. I made my way back into the hemlocks and cut uphill toward what has always been for me the heart of this particular piece of land. I stopped and picked up a scroll of white bark, dry and tightly curled.

Soon I came to the head of a bubbling spring. From a carpus of roots, mountain water spewed forth every season. Whenever I came, the spring was running. If the world was ending I could always count on finding sweet water here.

So it was that evening. I shoveled away dead leaves with my hands, careful not to sop myself, for it was growing cold. The spring gushed forth. I cupped my hands and drank and drank.

The forest dimmed. Above the spring I cleared the ground of twigs and hemlock needles and placed ten pieces of bluestone in a semicircular hearth. I ripped the birch bark into long ribbons; from a small tree I broke a handful of twigs and set them on top of the shredded bark. I gathered bigger branches and set them nearby.

I settled an arm's length from my tiny pyre. Before setting the match I waited. I studied the mass of black limbs blotting the moon brightening near its zenith. I tried to write some poetry, but it went nowhere. There was nowhere to go. The birch bark caught at once and it burned beautifully.

TO THE TOP OF
TABLE MOUNTAIN
WITH RANGER RUDGE

ON MAY 8, I spent the day with forest ranger Pat Rudge. It was a nasty morning—dark, rainy, and cold. Not the kind of day I would normally spend hiking; but that's what Rudge had in mind—a trek to the top of Table Mountain. We were to meet at Morra's store in Big Indian at 8:00 a.m. I bundled up and stuffed my day pack with extra shirts, a lunch that Rudge had told me over the phone to make sure was "hearty," a quart of water, and trappings of my trade—a pad, pens, and a camera.

On the way from Woodstock to Big Indian, rain snapped against the windshield. West of Shandaken, the mountains were shrouded in snow, which did not improve my disposition. At Morra's I poured myself coffee, took a seat on the porch, scanned the *Daily Freeman*, and waited for Rudge. Rain dripped off the eaves; the uplands looked frigid. I half hoped Rudge wouldn't show. Wishful thinking. A red Dodge pickup, with a camper shell and the Department of Environmental Conservation shield emblazoned on its side, pulled into the lot.

"All ready for a great day!" Rudge said as I hopped in the cab.

"Yup," I said with all the enthusiasm I could muster. We headed towards Oliveria.

Kicking around the Peekamoose, I had first met Rudge the previous spring. She came tromping down the road in her green ranger uniform carrying a full pack. Rudge has long chestnut hair and big green eyes. She is small, 5'3". We chatted about coyotes, cats, bears, topography, old routes spanning the Peekamoose and Denning Valleys, and illegal logging on state lands.

The shortwave radio in the truck squawked; Rudge squelched it. Between us on the bench-seat was a milk crate loaded with maps, tickets, permits (for camping and burning), and several hefty law books. Rudge told me she carried a gun. I asked her if she'd ever had to use it. "Not yet," she said. In the line of duty she'd never drawn it from the holster. The gun, the permits, the tickets, and the law books were all part of the enforcement end of her job. She'd bust people for burning without a permit, burning demolition material, cutting trees on state land, and illegal mining (removing, without permit, over 1,000 tons of soil in a calendar year).

As we drove through Oliveria, I was struck by the mix of impressions Rudge created. She was young, but exuded a quiet confidence. Gregarious, but seldom confiding, she had an official veneer, a set of responses for dealing with both the public and the press. But she was also direct, unassuming, and spontaneous. Raised in Stone Ridge, the fifth of six children, Rudge attended Catholic high school. Her father worked as a food salesman for Duso; her mother's a registered nurse. Rudge holds an Associates degree in fisheries and wildlife from the State University of New York in Cobleskill. After graduating, she worked for five years as a wildlife tech and three more as an assistant ranger before scoring high on the civil service exam; coincidentally a ranger position opened.

"I was lucky," Rudge admitted. Ranger jobs are hard to come by, and she landed herself a plum. Her territory (officially Region 3, township of Shandaken and the wilderness lands of Denning) covers the Burroughs Range (Slide, Cornell, and Wittenberg Mountains); the Bushwack Range (Lone, Balsam Cap, Rocky, Friday, and Table Mountains); a sixteen-mile stretch of trail that runs from Biscuit Creek to Pine Hill; Mount Tremper; Peekamoose and Table Mountains; the headwater and upper reaches of the Roundout and Espopus Creeks; and the east and west branches of the Neversink. In short, Rudge roams the heart of the southern Catskills, which, she and I agree, is probably the most pristine and stunning landscape aside from the Adirondacks in the state. What more could any ranger want?

"I'm not complaining," she said. "For me it's perfect." She was quick to add that not all rangers like to hike as much as she does. Some prefer the more social (and sedentary) end of the job, like filling out burn permits, which is what we were about to do.

We turned into the Catskill Mountain Lake House and were greeted by Mrs. Joedicke, an older woman in a house coat with a lilting accent and a twinkle in her eye. As Rudge filled out the permit, Joedicke told me that in 1961, when she was new in the valley, she accidently started a fire in the field behind the house. "We hadn't even been introduced to our neighbors yet," Joedicke said. "But we got an introduction fast when they all came running with buckets and shovels. We're glad and happy to have [Rudge] in the valley. When a woman takes that job she must have a special interest." In fact, Rudge is the only woman ranger in New York State.

We crested the pass at Winnisook into the snow which whisked down, settling on the forest floor and melting without trace into the black water of Winnisook Lake. Slide's unseen summit towered less than three miles away. Driving leisurely on County Route 47, we followed the west branch of the Neversink through Frost Valley into Denning. Rudge described a particularly dramatic search and rescue operation she'd mounted the previous August where lives had been at stake. A party of nine college freshmen from Columbia University planned to spend several days in the woods. Approaching Slide from Cornell, one member hurt his leg. "They were not psychologically or physically prepared," said Rudge.

After the accident, the kid buckled and couldn't walk. The group made its way to the cull between Slide and Cornell, half carrying the hobbled kid. Hurricane Josephine hit. Temperatures plummeted, and the wind raged. The group was equipped with light cotton clothing, tennis shoes, and a plastic sheet for shelter. Caught at over 3,000 feet, one of them in shock with hypothermia, they waited for help.

Rudge, her husband Bill (a forester with the DEC), an assistant, and ranger Bob Marrone started out on rescue in midafternoon. They had heard that the injury was a broken leg. The rescue team loped upstream to cover the distance to the cull in the shortest possible time. They arrived in early evening. Rudge said she felt like throttling the kid when she found out that he had only a twisted ankle. She administered first aid, left the group with provisions, and walked out over the top of Slide. She told the group to be packed and ready to go by ten the next morning when she'd arrive with a stretcher.

At 10 a.m. the group was in disarray. By the time they'd broken camp and started down the mountain, it was late in the day. Rudge followed the stream she had come up the day before, rotating four-man teams bearing the stretcher. It was still raining hard and cold with high winds and was "unbelievably foggy to boot." The stream had swelled to her hips; in the cavities the water was chest deep. The descent continued to nightfall. Everyone had hypothermia, and to this day, Rudge said, she's surprised no one drowned.

She finished the story as we arrived at the trail-head to the Denning lean-to. As we prepared to emerge from the truck, I kidded Rudge about her pack brimming with gear: radio, rations, medical kit, flashlight, extra socks, tarp, rain gear. It all adds up—the pack weighed twenty pounds.

"I get teased about my pack, but it saved my life," she said.

"Why?" I asked, though I already knew. I also knew Rudge was reluctant to talk about this.

"I was attacked by a grizzly. Without what's in here I'd be dead now."

We were out of the truck. Rudge had an abstracted scowl that wasn't directed at me exactly though I was well within its scope. "Where was this?" I asked about the grizzly, in spite of myself.

"Montana. I was day-hiking with a friend. He stalked us." Did the incident change her life? I asked. "It made me appreciate life more," she said, adding she'd never walk in grizzly country again. "Anyone who would is a damn fool. That's what I honestly think."

Talking about the incident fouled her mood. We took off through the upper reaches of the Tison Preserve toward the Denning lean-to campsite.

It feels good to be out, good to be walking. The forest is old hemlock, muffled, almost mute. Snow ticks softly to its floor. Rudge walks slightly behind me and to the side. My pace is faster than usual and slightly erratic. We hop through soft spots and skirt freshets that flood across the way. Rudge notes places on the trail that need work and mourns the overuse the area receives. Trillium are in bloom, with snow on the petals and waxy green leaves. I watch the way Rudge steps from stone to stone, leaving minimum evidence of her passage on a trail that without her I would kick along unwittingly.

The campsite is set high on the east branch of the Neversink, a stream that whips down from the cull between Slide and Cornell. High banks drop precipitously to a wide riverine flat. Like a switchyard, the stream branches into many channels, coiling through long ovals of woods before reconstituting and proceeding on its way to Denning.

A place of ambush, I think, but also a place conceived by a child's imagination—dike builder, dam builder, fashioner of complex irrigation systems, networks of aqueducts, rivulets among roots. The beavers have been at work with an ability for complex construction that mirrors our bifurcating abstractions. I feel the streams flowing backward to their source, where the builder and the thinker, the philosopher and engineer were not so far apart.

Crossing this intricate network of channels without soaking one's socks is no mean feat. Straddling a fallen tree, Rudge and I cross on our rears. She leads, scraping off the bulk of the snow. Rudge, who has carried her Fabiano leather hiking boots over her shoulder on the walk in, fords the next channel, immersed to the knees. I cross via another tree downstream. Rudge has been lobbying the DEC to put in bridges, and I have the feeling that one of the reasons she's brought me here is to publicize the cause. Changing her boots in the lean-to, she says, "I'd like to see this torn down." The structure is too close to the water, built in the '70s when DEC camping regulations were lax.

We cross more channels and start up into the mountains, rising out of hemlock into hardwood. Rudge occasionally reaches down and clears fallen limbs from the trail. The wind picks up as we gain elevation. Snow pelts our faces. I can't believe I am hiking in the middle of a blizzard on May 8. I trudge behind Rudge, placing my feet in her boot-prints. Her stride is long and unflagging; often she steps using only the toe of her boot, saving the trail. Our path traces the spine of Table Mountain as it rises from plateau to plateau. I occasionally glimpse Wildcat Mountain through the driving snow. Animal tracks cross our path; Rudge veers off to investigate.

"Coyote or dog and deer," she pronounces.

The tracks braid through the woods, disappearing into the Neversink ravine. It's an old story, I think, predator keen on scent of its prey.

"See. The deer is moving fast here!" Rudge squats and points to snow thrown out around the prints, scuffs and slashes in the leaf cover and dirt. We amble back to the trail of our own, an inch deep in snow, marked regularly by state blazes, wide as my desk, blatantly defined. We walk in silence, wrapped in thought, the meditative movement of footfall following footfall. Breath after breath mists the air before the abstracted masks of our faces.

Rudge stops us at a lookout on the edge of a fifty-foot bluff. Blueberry bushes bristle on the rocky ledge. Van Wyke's humped ridgeline emerges like a ghost. The wind whittles through my clothing.

"Do you want to continue?" she askes.

I ask how far it is to the summit. Another hour and a half at the pace we've been going, she says, intimating that alone she'd halve that time. It is tempting to turn aside and head down and away from the wind and cold. We've penetrated the heart of the southern Catskills and come to a place I've never been before. My nose runs and, though not cold, I feel light-headed and numb. Nevertheless, I want to go on, so we resume our climb.

Through the woods I hear water gurgling. We detour

to inspect a rare high-elevation spring frothing from the mountainside in all its glory. I drink deeply, the water very cold and flat.

Climbing again the balsam begin to appear, signifying that we have reached 3,500 feet. Table is just over 3,800 feet, so I know we don't have far to go. The balsam thickens: We are in the fairyland of the highest Catskill mountaintops. It is a world of dense miniatures: dwarf birches, wiry scrub, the lush balsam which suffuse the air with sweet-smelling sap. Bleached trunks of dead trees, mosses, and worn rocky outcrops appear primeval—untouched by the tanners and loggers, or the nineteenth-century pleasure-seekers who stripped the mountaintops for large-scale camping and panoramic views.

We stop at an orange metal box nailed to a ten-foot balsam perhaps a couple of hundred years old. It spreads a thick canopy of interwoven branches above us. The box is maintained by the 3,500 Club. The club's members have climbed all thirty-five Catskill peaks above 3,500 feet. Rudge would like to see the box go. She signs in Pat Rudge, Ranger. "To keep them honest," she says.

I clear a spot of snow on the trail out of the wind, plop down, and devour a meatloaf sandwich. Rudge, standing, eats bread she has baked herself and cheese. She's brought a thermos of steaming tea, not too sweet, and she offers me a cup which I gratefully accept. A luxury, the tea glows inside me.

We go back down the mountain chatting about home life (as seems appropriate for our return). Rudge, who has been married a year, says that she does the cooking. She and Bill have just bought a small house in Oliveria. He commutes an hour to New Paltz each day. After work, she runs or bikes for an hour. They have no television and spend evenings reading. In bed by ten, they're up at six, when she makes breakfast.

Rudge asks me not to mention the incident with the grizzly. I ask why.

"I've dealt with it, my family's dealt with it," she says and adds that she doesn't want to be known as the ranger who was attacked by a grizzly. She's been burned by journalists before. One man who interviewed her called the hospital in Montana where she spent five weeks recuperating to get her medical report.

"Just try to be gentle," she adds.

Back at the lean-to, I ask Rudge about *Giardia*, small parasites that live in water and cause stomach problems. "I wouldn't drink the water. It's definitely here." I tell her that I grew up in the Catskills drinking water from the upland streams and ask why things have changed.

"People," she says.

Recrossing a rushing channel I nearly slip on a slick log. Rudge reaches out and grabs my hand. We do our tree-straddling dance at the next crossing. I go first and turn the camera on Rudge, endearingly mortified and full of laughter as she bumps across.

It is late afternoon, and I'm glad to be back in the truck heading home. Rudge stops at the YMCA's Denning Estate to fill out a camping permit for a group of senior citizens who plan to spend the night at the lean-to. We drive back through Denning and head up the pass to Big Indian.

On the way, we spot a station wagon with New Jersey plates. It pulls into a turn-off on state land. Rudge decides to check it out.

"Just here to do a little fishing," says a wiry man in his early forties with a pencil-thin mustache. He wears a camouflage jacket, gold chains, and a gold watch. Rudge and I look at each other.

"That's allowed, isn't it?" he says.

"Sure is," says Rudge. "How long are you going to be here?"

"Oh, we're just up for the afternoon."

A burly younger man, in jeans with half-laced workman's boots, emerges from behind the station wagon. Rudge asks them to make sure not to litter.

"What do you think?" she says as we pull out.

"I don't know."

"I don't know either."

The front wheels of the Dodge sink into a slough of deep mud. Rudge puts the truck into four-wheel drive, but the spinning wheels, like a man struggling in quicksand, simply serve to send us deeper in the muck. I jump out and push as Rudge rocks, but we are mired to the front axle. The mustached man and his buddy arrive. Rudge has a winch which we connect to the back of their station wagon. As we are winched out the mustached man and his friend chortle. In Rudge's place, I would probably feel embarrassed, but she handles the situation with aplomb.

"Been stuck before, and I'll be stuck again," she says as we drive away.

At Slide Mountain trail-head, Rudge changes the ranger's message tablet in the information center. The old message reads "Ice above 3,600 feet, crampons necessary. Fire danger below."

"What should I write?" Rudge cogitates with a responsible air. After a minute, in a clear hand with a red marker, she writes: "High water at the East Branch of the Neversink. Caution crossing."

It is almost five p.m., and suddenly, standing in the lot, I feel tired and chilled. Rudge comes and stands next to me. We stand in silence a moment, feeling the evening deepen. She can see I'm through.

"Time to call it a day," she says, and we head over the pass into Oliveria.

TO FURLOUGH LODGE

At Furlough Lodge the rich are not so idle. Everybody dashes about as though late for an urgent appointment. Activity predominates. Little Chappy tumbles down the stairs and out the door. He's off to sail the lake with a slew of cavorting siblings and cousins. A horse-drawn cart shoots across the lawn commandeered by a small girl in a wide-brimmed hat. Children frisk on a shoreside trampoline. The clay tennis court is empty, but not for long. After lunch it will be the scene of an unending carousel of round-robin doubles.

Kingdon Gould Jr., age sixty-six, father of nine and grandfather of twenty-three, is the patriarch of all this purposeful vivacity. His deeply tanned forearms ripple with muscle. His eyes are a hard clear blue. When he stares at me the corners of his mouth occasionally twitch upwards in a cold parody of a smile. When more genuinely amused he projects a distant appreciation.

Gould is one of the largest private landowners in the Catskills. He owns 5,000 acres in Dry Brook (a long valley winding south out of Arkville), which includes most of Graham and Doubletop Mountains. The valley forms a cul-de-sac at the base of Doubletop, affording almost absolute privacy. The estate boasts numerous outbuildings; some are used by family members, others rented.

Our initial interview takes place in the library, a long, thin room with trophies on the wall and a big stone fireplace. The lodge itself is rambling but not palatial. Built of logs, it is modeled on an Adirondack great camp. After seating me in an elaborately carved chair, Gould asks me about myself. When I mention that I taught English in Japan, he says that he wanted to buy the dramatic rights to *Iron and Silk* by Mark Salzman, who, just out of Yale, taught English in China while studying martial arts. He tracked Salzman to Hollywood and phoned, only to find him already embarked on just such a project. Gould indicates that the martial-arts angle of Salzman's China experience hooked him.

Charles Lancaster, Gould's grandson, enters. He's fourteen, soft-spoken, and watchful. We shake hands. Gould asks him to carry money to one of the organizers of the community hall square dance that night which the family plans to attend. Charles exits and Gould and I discuss Dry Brook. He mentions that one of his sons was married in the local church.

I say that I'd imagined him at a remove, cloistered on his private estate; but from what I gather it seems that he's locally involved.

"Well, I hope so. We'll have the neighborhood up for the Fourth of July fireworks, as is our custom. I like to think we're part of the overall scene."

Charles drifts back into the room. "Mind if I listen?" he asks. Gould waves him to a low sofa that projects a well-worn rustic opulence, the lodge's overall feel.

Gould can't remember the exact number of his grandchildren. Twenty-two, he thinks, "A pretty numerous lot.

All extremely well behaved." He refers the question to Charles, who shrugs. "Twenty-two or twenty-three," he says. "Although it doesn't really matter."

"It does to the twenty-third," jokes Gould.

Charles leaves. Upstairs I hear women, a suggestion of billowing sheets, cloth snapping and folding, light footsteps moving to and fro—the Gould animation distilling the late morning into a clean-burning fuel.

Other members of the family come tripping in, singly and in groups. I meet Charles's mother, Candida, who is roughly my age, freckled, and wears her frizzy hair pulled back. I shake hands with half a dozen other grandchildren.

Gould's son Frank pops in for a brief hello. Fortyish, intent, with a conspiratorial wink, he wants to hear about the book in which his father will be featured. He asks how I started writing. I reply that I began with poetry. I want to add that I branched out to pay the bills, but the subject is tacitly dropped. A keenness hones from Frank as he says "See you later" and departs.

Charles sidles back toward the sofa. "Twenty-three grandchildren," he reports.

"Thank you, Charles. It's good to know."

The phone rings. Gould answers it himself in the adjoining room.

"What do you think about vacationing here?" I ask Charles.

"Pretty darn lucky. Some people sit around and watch television all summer."

Gould replaces the receiver and resumes his seat. Our discussion turns to the Catskills and yields no surprises. Addressing the need for conservation, Gould says development is also necessary. "It's all very well for people, how should I say, who don't earn their livelihood here to protest development."

The Goulds, in fact, have long been an important part of the Dry Brook economy. In Norman Studer's book

A Catskill Woodsman: Mike Todd's Story, Waldron Dumond recounts the ambivalence—a mix of resentment and dependency—that the Gould influx of money produced in Dry Brook at the end of the last century:

> After the Gould people came in, they hired everybody in the valley, practically everybody worked for Gould, and the farms went to pot. He took a 200 foot strip along the streams, but they still had their farms and worked for him. When George Gould [Kingdon Jr.'s, grandfather] died they had to come back to the farming, then some 'em did have quite a time keeping alive.

Dumond doesn't mention that the failure of dairying was a regional, rather than a local, phenomenon. Apropos, as we continue talking, Gould mourns that none of the forty-four dairy farms in the Dry Brook area at the close of World War II remain. Mentioning a preference for open land, he says he runs 200 head of beef cattle and pastures "pleasure ponies for the girls." He scoffs at Catskill springs (too wet and muddy) and criticizes New York City's unfair reservoir "impoundment" regulations; he detects opportunities for small businessmen and creative people to locate here using telecommunications.

I've been increasingly distracted by the numerous trophies mounted on the walls. I ask Gould if he hunts.

"It's become harder and harder for me to shoot anything," he replies. "Something about the process of growing up. You become more concerned about taking another life. Now I prefer to fish with a barbless hook."

It seems Gould, who is beginning to warm a bit, has hit his stride. I sense I should sit still—but I feel restless, tired with talk. And Gould obviously prefers to remain private. He's set the conversation on an arid plateau that is as flat as his speech. I feel a peculiar numbness. Snapping closed my pad, I ask permission to stroll around.

Gould says he'd like to give me a sandwich in an hour and directs me on a loop. He insists that I look inside the estate's old icehouse, confessing that the use to which he's put it makes him inordinately proud. I remind him that when he wrote inviting me to visit he said to bring a fishing rod. I ask if I can fish after lunch; he hesitates before agreeing on the condition that I release whatever I catch.

First I call home. The beat-up black rotary phone is in the living room—a large, shadowy space cluttered with relics. A polar bear rug is spread on the floor at my feet, the bear's tongue protrudes from its mouth as though panting. I reach down and it comes loose in my hand. It is tuberous and dense, and its fleshy nodules feel slick as wax. Gould checks in and says something like "the old boy's decomposing." On the way out I pass the help sweeping up mountain laurel blossoms that have fallen to the floor from a large bouquet set in a vase by the lodge's main stairway.

Gould's great-grandfather, Jay Gould, was born in Roxbury, a hop, skip, and a jump from the lodge. He and John Burroughs were childhood friends. The son of a poor farmer, Gould had written a history of Delaware County by the time he was twenty. By thirty he had made his fortune, and at forty he was one of the richest men in the country. He made his initial money during the Civil War, reaping the rewards of the North's rapid industrial growth. After the war, he invested in railroads and the telegraph. Like his great-grandson, he was a small, wiry man with indefatigable energy. Accounts portray him as a merciless businessman, astute almost to prescience, and a devoted family man. Like John Rockefeller, Andrew Carnegie, Cornelius Vanderbilt, and J. P. Morgan, Gould has been branded a "robber baron." The term is medieval, referring to large landowners who fleeced travelers passing through their realms.

Matthew Josephson's book *The Robber Barons* appeared in 1934. His Depression-era portrait of Gould is particularly scathing: It affirmed Joseph Pulitzer's assessment of Gould as "one of the most sinister figures that ever flitted bat-like across the vision of the American people." Josephson's book casts Gould as the anti-Christ in the Great American capitalist allegory of success— where a nobody from nowhere makes millions, and his children marry the royal blood of Europe.

But a recent major work questions the popular assumptions about Gould. *The Life and Legend of Jay Gould* by Maury Klein, a professor of history at the University of Rhode Island, is a revisionist tome. Klein's Gould is a brilliant if ruthless businessman whose nefarious image was the result of press hype:

> Looked at with a sense of detachment, Gould's business ethics were probably no worse and in some respects better than those of most men. What separated him from others was not his dishonesty but his talent, his daring, his sense of vision. He took great risks and stood behind them. He was quick to change his mind but not at the expense of abandoning an ally or a commitment. No man who was his friend need fear for his wallet; no man who was his foe dared sleep at his post.

Klein's text is steeped in the pervasive metaphors of a market economy as game or war. His assessment of Gould seems as much a product of the Reagan era as Josephson's is of the Depression. Edwin Hoyt and Richard O'Connor, in the '60s, the era of the great society question why Gould (like Rockefeller or Carnegie) was relatively unconcerned with public works.

Whatever Jay Gould's business ethics, everyone agrees

that he loved his family. He had six children. The eldest, George (Kingdon Jr.'s grandfather), comes off as something of a dilettante, doomed to live forever in his father's shadow. In 1904, George wrote "Polo and the Business-man," an article for the *Independent*. He was an avid yachtsman. Instead of minding the family money, he was given to gallivanting about Europe. One biographer declares that he lacked the aggression and acumen of his sire. Another says he was brilliant but lazy. His Georgian Court at Lakewood, New Jersey, had the reputation as the "most magnificent private residence" in the country. George bought the acreage around Furlough Lake and built the lodge in 1890.

Jay Gould's other children led the lives, in their own fashion, of second-generation American wealth: Helen Gould, a strict pro-abolitionist, was devout and gave large amounts of money to good works. Her retreat in Roxbury, Kirkside, is now a home for the elderly. Anna Gould married European nobility—twice—and lived much of her life in France. Frank Gould was a prodigious dissolute until his middle years, when he apparently straightened up and made an immense fortune in his own right. Edwin Gould was quiet and reclusive, a prudent investor; he had a home in Rhinebeck.

The eldest of ten children, Kingdon Gould's father, Kingdon Sr., was educated by tutors. He received a degree in mining engineering from Columbia in 1909. He directed several railroad companies that had been in the family since Jay Gould's day: the Denver and Rio Grande, Missouri Pacific, Western Pacific, and Texas and Pacific. Like his grandfather, he played an active role in Western Union Telegraph Company. He expanded the family's mining operations. During World War I, Kingdon Sr. entered the army as a private and was awarded two commendations for action in the Argonne Forest. He was fluent in Italian, French, Spanish, German, and Arabic. He married an

Italian, Annunziata Camilla Maria, daughter of Candido Lucci of Arezzo. Late in life, he became a practicing Roman Catholic. Politically, he was a Republican. Like his father, he was an avid fisherman and polo player. He died in 1945.

Kingdon Jr. was born in 1924, the only boy of three children. One of his sisters, still living, resides part time in Kings Lodge, Dry Brook. Gould received his B.A. from Yale and entered military service in 1942 as a private, like his father. Released in 1946 as a second lieutenant, he had received battlefield commissions and been awarded two Silver Stars and two Purple Hearts. In 1946, he married Mary Thorne. After receiving his LL.B. from Yale in 1951, he set up a private practice. For one year he was the Finance Chairman of Maryland's Republican Party. From 1969 to 1972, Gould served as Ambassador to Luxembourg and from 1973 to 1976 as Ambassador to the Netherlands.

Washington Post articles from 1973 report that due to large contributions to Nixon's campaign, the senate raised ethical questions during Gould's appointment hearings for the Netherlands post. He reappeared in the press again in 1978, petitioning officials for retaliatory trade sanctions after Panama nationalized a 500,000-acre plantation which Gould owned with Dominic Antonelli, his partner in Washington parking and real estate interests. Gould then seems to have vanished from the public eye, although his connections and great wealth make him an extremely influential man.

I start my walk toward the icehouse. Gould doesn't conform to my stereotype of a diplomat. It's tough picturing him in black tie, presiding at diplomatic functions. Not only his clothes (shorts, a worn red shirt, and sandals), but also his bearing seems unsuited for the role.

Reconciliation and negotiation seem foreign for him, the distance between what he thinks and says too thin. He buffers himself with his family, too private for such a public role. His dignity lacks grace; but perhaps that's only his response to me or his Catskill manner—an air he assumes when not absorbed in what may be an intensely social Washington life.

Trout feed by the lake's outlet; clear water rolls languidly over a stone spillway. I wander into the mossy woods by the lake's edge. A sailboat scoots before a breeze that raises welts on the water's ebony skin. The day is cool and damp. A swimming float rocks thirty feet from shore. Earlier I had been introduced to six-year-old Camilla (one of the twenty-three grandchildren) who swam around the float and back for the first time that very morning to pass her swimming test. She would now be allowed to brave the lake without her swimmie, a floatation device worn around the waist. She nodded her head shyly, eyes aglow, when Gould proclaimed the good news.

Charles rolls by in an American-made station wagon on his way to deliver money to the estate foreman for the dance. I ask if he would take me fishing after lunch, and he agrees.

I lope down the road. The woods are carefully tended, pruned, open, and park-like. I take a shortcut. The ferns and tall grass are sopped from morning rain, and my tan boot leather is soon splotched with brown. I pass neatly stacked woodpiles and a wire enclosure around a satellite dish in a boggy glade. The foreman's house is fronted by pasture; there are beautiful views. Nearby, horses graze around a large white barn. I hop a fence and skid down a steep bank to the icehouse.

The structure is brown stone, tall and round. Hoofs have trampled its muddy periphery. Manure smell clots the air. Gould has piqued my curiosity, and I tug at a back door, which is loose on its hinges but locked. I circle to the front. Potted flowers flank a flagstone stoop, and three narrow windows ascend above a neatly painted door. Across a gravel roadway is a large riding arena set up with colorful hurdles. The ensemble could have been conceived by Magritte: the off-kilter specificities in a manicured landscape.

The surrealism of the scene heightens as I enter the icehouse. Gould has turned it into a squash court. On either side of the foyer, doors lead into the dead space between the interior box and its circular housing. The clammy air is ripe with dirt, sawdust, and mildew. I feel as though I'm in a bathysphere. I climb a narrow flight of stairs and contemplatively linger on an upstairs balcony with a view of the empty court. When I click my tongue, echoes ricochet off the ceiling and walls. Red lines in the burnished floor indicate the game's geometry. Though unoccupied, the structure expresses its function.

I'm beginning to zone. Rousing myself, I continue walking downhill past the riding arena. Soon I approach an artificial lake fronting a rambling blue house. Later I learn it's called *Vlyvaal* ("fly valley," in Dutch), once the Fairbairn Farm, home to Gould's uncle, then occupied by Sylvia Romilly, Gould's deceased sister, now rented.

The road winds upward. I quicken my pace, concerned that I have loitered in the icehouse too long. When I near a jeep wagon with attached horse trailer parked in front of a stone garage, I'm not sure exactly where I am. A grassy swath forms a carpet leading to a large house perhaps a hundred yards distant. It seems I've stumbled on another of the estate's residences. Should I introduce myself and see if they bear any relation to the Goulds? An older man wearing a cloth hat emerges. There is something familiar in his posture, his isolation, the intensity with which he scrutinizes his tennis racket. Then all at once it hits me: It's Gould himself!

What was completely alien a moment before shifts back to the familiar. There are the American cars (new but not particularly ostentatious) in the driveway. There is the lakeside trampoline with its eternally bouncing squadron. That is the tennis court which I passed on my way into the house (although from another angle). The display resolves itself; and with it comes attendant hesitations. I tread toward the lodge almost against my will.

I find Gould in the laundry room where a big washer-dryer does double duty. He ushers me through the house and deposits me on a stone patio overlooking the lawn and lake. A small group of men and women in their thirties and forties are eating sandwiches and making conversation. The atmosphere is casual. I grab a sandwich wrapped in plastic from a large basket, and Candida fetches me a drink.

Gould's wife, Mary, strides up the lawn all *joie de vivre*. She could be a stand-in for Katherine Hepburn: the same teased hair, high cheekbones, strong jaw, freckled skin, society accent, breezy affect, and airy charm. She is almost as deeply tanned as Gould. Where Gould is dense and opaque, she is bright and almost transparent: they complement each other. She asks about my walk and leans forward with a "do tell" aspect when I report that I saw two youngish men at *Vlyvaal*.

Gould comes from the house and takes a seat. "What's it to be this afternoon, gentlemen?" he queries, wolfing down his sandwich. "Golf, tennis, or fishing?" The gentlemen include Frank and a large fair man from the Netherlands, Frans Van Wagenberg.

"You're unbelievable, Mr. Gould!" says Van Wagenberg's wife Amal, a dark, vivid Kuwaiti. Gould favors her with an uncomprehending expression. "You're always going. You never stop!" she continues.

"You only live once," Mary Gould spurts gaily. "You

might as well enjoy it. Can't do anything when you're dead."

Frank says he wants to present his father with a large print of a photograph taken while they were mountain climbing in South America. It is difficult to tell if Gould likes the idea. Frank then says something about wanting to run Graham and Doubletop. It comes out that father and son made a similar run—forty miles—although Gould admits that they covered part of the course in a stagger rather than a sprint. This information is conveyed in a very understated, almost muddled, style (which could pass for modesty if luncheon conversation were confined to feats of prowess). Frank does the talking with Gould occasionally inserting a clipped comment. The women are duly impressed, as am I.

Gould again tries to rally support for the afternoon's activities. We look at the sky and discuss the weather. He asks about my plans. I say that I've made arrangements with Charles to go fishing, so off we go in search of Charles.

We find him enveloped by an entourage of young male cousins. Charles leads me into the "sports room" and unpacks his fly-tying apparatus.

"What kind of fly do you want?" he asks.

We discuss hackles, deer hair, and colored threads. When he learns that I don't tie my own flies, he becomes less self-conscious.

The younger cousins catapult into the room. The eldest, Matteo Barbieri from Pisa (ten years old, dark, and thin as a bean) calls for a game of Masters and Slaves.

"What's a slave?" asks little Chappy, Frank's son.

"A slave is a worker who has to do whatever his master says and is whipped and beaten," replies the salivating Matteo.

"No," says Charles, barely looking up from his work. "A slave is someone who works for someone else without pay. That's all."

Little Chappy soon finds out what slavery, economic and otherwise, is all about. His cousins pin him to a couch in the middle of the room and nearly suffocate him with pillows.

When no sound has come from the weakly writhing Chappy for a couple of minutes, Charles intercedes. He cools Chappy's "masters" with a soft rebuff. They appear to have been waiting for his word and emancipate Chappy instantly. He howls and sets upon his tormenters with a volley of fists. Charles, peering through a six-inch magnifying glass attached on a crane to the table, barely bats an eye. He finishes one fly and starts on another.

A big-bodied blond woman strides into the room dressed in tennis whites. "I'm Susan Gould," she says and holds out her hand. She is Frank's wife, Chappy's mother. As we talk it turns out she is interested in poetry. Before exiting, she reads aloud to the children at high speed, from a picture book on Egyptian mummies. They raptly absorb the tale of embalmment and burial with priceless dynastic possessions, of kings that eternally rule in the land of the dead.

Finished with the flies, Charles puts his gear together for our expedition while I watch Frank and the Dutchman take on Gould and Susan in doubles tennis. Frank, who after lunch neatly groomed the clay court, has a powerful backhand. Gould plays hard, with total concentration. His game is good although not expert. The Dutchman makes a series of splendid shots. Gould retaliates in a furor of competitive fever. Frank smashes a return at his wife at net.

The day is overcast and cool. Charles and I drive to *Vlyvaal*. I ask about his family. He says his father, Charles Calvert Lancaster II, recently managed the Peabody Bookshop in Baltimore. He is working at the moment and so can't join them. The Lancasters vacation every other summer in the Catskills. Odd summers they gather elsewhere.

We arrive at the lake, and Charles pulls a canoe through the mowed grass to the water's edge. We push off and he paddles us to the mouth of a small stream. "This is the second best spot," he says, maneuvering the bow twenty feet away and broadside to trout rising in a shallow inlet. He hands me his Orvis rod baited with a streamer. "Cast along the shore," he directs.

After my first few casts, he asks if I've ever fished in this way. I haven't. He instructs me to keep the streamer moving and points out what to look for when the fish strike.

I soon hook several six- to ten-inch brookies and pass the rod to Charles. He expertly peels line off the reel. His casts are effortless and exact.

We wet our hands, extracting the barbs and releasing our prey as gently as possible. Charles spends several minutes working loose a hook after a small fish takes a fly deep into its gullet. Finally free, the fish hangs in the water sideways for a full minute before righting itself and wavering slowly into the coppery depths.

So far Charles has been unerringly polite, diffident, reserved, and older than his fourteen years. At times he is almost grave. We arrive at the number-one fishing spot, a narrow estuary sluicing into the underbrush. A deep channel hugs the left bank. Charles offers me the rod. I tell him to go ahead, that I enjoy watching him fish. He takes pleasure from the comment and casts with aplomb, holding the rod in his lap. Except for the wrist, his arm barely moves. The line flows out thirty feet and then drops into the water gently, fully extended, without a splash. I'm all admiration.

I ask Charles about his interests. "Do you mean: 'What I want to be when I grow up?' " he asks, slightly peeved. I reply that I'm curious about what gives him pleasure, how he spends his time, and how he views his life.

The testiness evaporates. He says he enjoys making

things, working with his hands. He's thought about becoming an architect. He likes to fish. I tell him fishing stories set in Alaska and the Himalayas and about two long canoe trips I took through northern Canada. We hook and free more fish: then Charles says it is time to get back to the lodge where he's promised to take Chappy sailing.

Back at the lodge, I watch Gould still scampering about the tennis court. I feel he wants to wear himself down to a battered nub, a satiety of endeavour, so that he knows he's used himself to the fullest and has no more to give. He also wants to win. When Susan errs there is a touch of asperity as he receives her apology.

Between games, as the players change sides, I say goodbye.

"Thank you for thinking of us," calls Gould, taking his position on the baseline. With a grunt, clenched jaw, and rictus of muscles he stretches himself to full height and comes slamming down on his serve.

I return to the lodge later that summer to take photographs and ask Gould some follow-up questions. It's a sparkling morning. Gould and his wife are without guests. The house, in contrast to my last visit, is very quiet. I sit with my wife and new-born son, who nurses, at the breakfast table. Gould serves us coffee, which is mellow and thick. The table still holds the remains of the morning meal: pretty china, egg cups, a small glass jar of homemade preserves, and bran muffins.

From the first, though not exactly ebullient, Gould is almost affable, friendlier and more relaxed than at our previous meeting. He seems pleased with the baby's presence, the glorious morning, and the serenity which reigns at the lodge. He is full of boyish expressions—'Holy Toledo!'' he exclaims at one point. I ask him a string of factual questions. Mrs. Gould enters and sits with us. Her underlying attitude is protective, skeptical, and impatient; she distrusts the press. Outwardly, she is tough, girlish, and charming.

I ask Gould about the resolution of his Panama venture. He said at the time the new Canal treaty was signed, all land claims were resolved. Mrs. Gould says the treaty was "one of the stupidest things our government has ever done." Gould agrees. I question him about his role in the Republican Party; he replies that he has none. We go on to discuss the issues that he faced as a diplomat.

During Gould's Luxembourg tenure, the Common Market (then only six countries) was expanding. The big question was whether or not Great Britain would join. Luxembourg was an ideal post from which to report on developments—the European Court and Parliament rotated between there and Strasbourg. It was Europe in miniature, and the people speak three languages: French, German, and Luxembourgish.

My wife, a German scholar, intercedes and asks about Luxembourgish, which Gould says the citizens would "hate to see described as a dialect." He adds, "The country was very generous to Americans. Eight of the ten largest companies were American. Du Pont, Uni Royal, Goodyear all had large manufacturing operations. Luxembourg sought investment, which proved very beneficial both from the companies' and Luxembourg's perspective."

The Netherlands post was very different. The Vietnam War had turned the Dutch press into the most anti-American of any country in western Europe. The Netherlands had a tremendous American investment: $9 billion in plants and installations. Only Singapore is a more densely populated country, so the Dutch developed an early environmental awareness. They had sophisticated ideas about land use which Gould found interesting. Rotterdam was the largest port in the world by some fifty percent. At the end of his tenure he said anti-American feeling had "ameliorated substantially." Gould said that he interpreted Nixon's resignation for the Dutch, who wanted to know if the event heralded a shift away from a strong executive branch.

When Nixon announced his resignation, Chief Justice Warren Burger was a Gould house guest at the Embassy in the Hague. Gerald Ford wanted to make sure Burger would swear him in. "We had quite a time getting him back" reminisced Mrs. Gould. "The call came at two a.m. We put him on the plane at four a.m. As soon as he finished the swearing-in, he hopped on a plane and came back to finish his vacation."

I ask Gould what he felt when Nixon resigned. He says that he thought it was important that the transition took place in a civil proceeding and that it was "an amazing fact that America continued as it always had...I thought [Nixon] was a good president from an international relations point of view."

I've finished my questions and ask to take photos; Mrs. Gould is not enthused. The lodge's interior is off-limits; it is a jumble of mismatched artifacts. In fact, she prefers that I not take photos at all; the lodge is a country retreat, the family's getaway, a private place where they escape the world. I press the issue. Finally, she relents and I take exterior shots. Then she reluctantly accompanies Gould to the rolling lawn that stretches from the house to the lake.

Gould sports a cap and a blue blazer with a crest on its breast pocket. He puts his arm around her, tilts his chin upward, and smiles at the distance. She squirms. I take several shots. They are a handsome couple and present a picture of a marriage that has worked.

We seem to have reached a truce as Mrs. Gould walks with us to our car before going to feed the horses. Gould sputters up in a red Triumph sports car, its engine cold. He has to see about a new well for *Vlyvaal* and will drop his wife at the barn.

Driving down the long private roads bordered by miles of beautiful wooden fencing, my wife remarks on what a good-looking man Gould is and says she liked Mrs. Gould. We talk about class and privilege, business and politics, inadequacy and condescension, democracy and dynasty, communication and rote response, privacy and journalistic ethics. "I couldn't believe you persisted about the pictures," she says, as though my pushiness approached that of Genghis Khan.

I think that the photos were like the last lunge in a fencing match, or a difficult move on a rock face—once you commit, you're committed. We drive the length of the Dry Brook Valley. The "no trespassing" signs go on for miles. They are signed, "Kingdon Gould, Arkville."

MEN WHO OWN MOUNTAINS: NELSON SHULTIS

NELSON SHULTIS BECAME a lumberman—like his father, his grandfather, and his great-grandfather. He owned and operated the Wittenberg sawmill until 1984, when he sold it to Aaron Van De Bogart III. Van De Bogart ran the mill for a few years and then sold it to the people who run the Wittenberg Center for Alternative Resources—a new-age operation that specializes in father-son sweat lodge retreats and shamanistic workshops. Today the old red mill buildings stand idle, their airy interiors filled with dusty light that seems to hold the residue of searing saws.

The Shultis family lived in Wittenberg for four generations. But in the 1960s, Nelson moved from the family homestead to the almost 3,000 acres in the heart of the southern Catskills that he bought piecemeal, beginning in 1958 with an 1,800-acre purchase. He recently sold 2,000 of these acres to the State because his taxes were running at $22,000 a year. Retired now, he can't afford the burden. He's kept the 900 acres located in the township of Olive where, he says, taxes are reasonable.

Shultis is in his seventies and wears a hearing aid, testimony to his days around sawmills and chain saws. Under medium height, he's stocky but not burly. He moves well for his age, in fact like a much younger man. He generally wears some form of headgear, from white plastic hard hats to John Deere felt-rimmed tractor caps with plastic ventilator webbing above the ears. The hats cover scant white hair. His round face ranges from a stolid indifference (which is really his way of being polite) to a kind of impishness—quick to excite, quick to instruct. He has a fraternal gregariousness without a speck of pretense and the independent air of a self-made man.

Shultis is a hunter who eats what he kills—bear, deer, and wild turkey. He likes to fish and has fished his whole life. He used to trap—mink, fox, and coon—and still lays out an occasional line, last year with his grandson. He keeps a large garden and puts up food for the winter. He makes maple syrup and once made it in volume, but recently sold his evaporator. He once kept bees. He owns a maddening array of vehicles and machinery over which he is constantly dickering. And he knows the eastern Catskills as well as any man alive.

One of the last of his generation, Shultis represents the kind of man who used to call these mountains home. He also represents a type of relationship to the land—a stewardship that is changing from private to state hands. Most of the remaining men who own large chunks of Catskill land belong to the wealthy landed gentry—men like Laurence Rockefeller, Kingdon Gould, and Howard Pack. But Shultis does not fit into this group. He's worked all his life with his hands. And he's made a living, not a fortune, working the land.

I visited Shultis one morning in mid-September. He had just returned from Cape Cod and was busy making stuffed clams. The immediate vicinity around his house was full of machinery, vehicles in varying states of disrepair, a couple of trailers, an American flag on a pole surrounded by flowers, horseshoes nailed to the side of half a dozen outbuildings, several neatly stacked woodpiles as long as tractor trailers, an old plow, and a couple of empty wire traps.

Shultis told me that he moved up to this place to get away from people telling him what he can and cannot do; he left Woodstock for just that reason. "Won't let you do anything there!" he said, fed up but not in the least embittered. Shultis pointed to the waterfall, pretty as a picture behind his house. The view of the falls from his back porch is the reason he picked the spot.

Directly below the porch were the remains of what Shultis told me had been two charcoal kilns. We talked about how charcoal was made in the late nineteenth century after the hemlock and the tanners were gone. Axmen worked for a dollar a day; the charcoal was strictly hardwood—wood fiber with all the acids slowly burned out, a process which in the old kilns took about a week. Shultis said charcoal, tended right, burns as hot as coal.

He asked if I'd like to see the remains of the other kilns up in the woods. When I said I would, he backed a roofless, battered jeep out of its stall. We bounced over a small stream and up a rocky road.

"Wouldn't know these woods been lumbered, would you?" Shultis asked. Open woods, green ground cover, and the fox-silver trunks of maple rising up and up. Aside from an occasional stump, no, I couldn't tell. Selective cutting, he explained with pride.

After a mile or so he stopped the jeep. We waded through a thick berry patch, thorns ripping at my arms, green tendrils curling over my head. Crashing through stubborn vegetable sinew the air was minty, mixed with musk rising from the ground. We shadowed a faint game trail, Shultis ahead, swimming through the tangle. Just off the trail, he pointed to fresh bear scat rife with berry seeds.

We broke from briars high on a shallow brook tumbling over mossy stones. A fallen branch foiled the remnants of a crossing. Two streams joined in a shallow pool where Shultis insisted trout lurked. Of trout I saw neither fin nor scale; instead, I saw slick stones at strange angles with the deadfall blocking access to the opposite bank. Shultis egged me on, encouraging me to cross and get the best shot of the kiln up the far bank—a dismal ruin not in the least picturesque.

Fording the stream was even trickier than it first appeared, with Shultis a safe spectator at the stream's edge saying "watch yourself"; I tried to minimize my klutziness hauling myself up the slippery stone by grabbing the deadfall's branches, which felt like they were going to give at any moment. Such a small thing but nonetheless complex. Once across, I looked back for some kind of affirmation only to find that Shultis had silently vanished into the woods.

I squatted on the flat dry stone for which I'd worked so hard and savored the newness of the place, the loneliness, and the quiet. I sat for perhaps five minutes and then recrossed easily, further downstream, to find Shultis sitting in the jeep, waiting.

As we headed back to the house, Shultis pointed out trees: maple, maple, maple—ninety-nine percent maple here, he said. He gestured towards the occasional white oak, ash, or beech and told me that basswood honey, from the small white basswood flowers, is delicious. "That's some delicious honey," he said.

Everything was wet and glistening from the morning rain. A red-tail hawk hovered, flush against the dome of Blackberry Mountain. Insects with wings of pale green rode the thick river of light pouring through the forest into the clearing, over the grasses and nettles and ferns.

Shultis promised to take me up to one of his private hunting lodges and a couple of weeks later, I'm back at his place. When I arrive it is 2 p.m.; I'm ten minutes late. Before I can say hello, Shultis has the jeep turned around, sputtering like a spitfire, pointing uphill. Strapped to the dash is a .22-magnum with a telescopic sight; two chain saws are fitted in a built-in wood box in the rear. Shultis has donned his white plastic hard hat.

When he sold off his 2,000 acres to the state, Shultis kept a hunting lodge which he had built, surrounded by ten acres. He has a right-of-way to and from the lodge for twenty years; then the lodge and acreage will revert to the state.

We take the same road past the last of the old kilns and the berry patch and continue on roads that Shultis built with a bulldozer when he was still lumbering. The day is cool and clear. As we climb, Shultis puts the jeep in low; its wheels spin and catch. I'm pushed into the seat with my head thrown back, like riding up the initial grade of a roller coaster.

The jeep whines and Shultis nurses it up the harrowing grade with cheerful aplomb. He's spent a lifetime building and negotiating logging roads, and he's clearly in his element and enjoying himself. I grip the dash, remembering that the jeep is roofless because—as Shultis, deadpan, pointed out before our first excursion—two of his workers lost their brakes coming down this very mountain.

We approach a particularly ghoulish turn. "All paid up," Shultis says with his impish grin. "Tricky spot," he admits, as we slowly roll back toward an abyss.

After a bit more of these shenanigans, we near the top of the bowl. The road levels and loops. The trees are smaller, predominantly beech and birch. Still climbing, but gradually, I begin to see that we are skirting the rim of a high cirque. To the north and west, Shultis points out the humps of Cornell, Balsam Cap, and Lone Mountains. To the east, the long flank of Hanover stretches toward the glimmer of a corner of the Ashokan Reservoir.

Shultis points to black marks on the beech. "What's that?" he challenges. "You grew up on Hutchin Hill." I have to admit I don't know. Shultis tells me that bear make the marks climbing the young beech to get the beech nut. As the trees age, the marks remain. I can see claw prints clearly defined in the bark.

Even this high, and on the north side of the mountain, the leaves are just beginning to turn. We drive slowly over trickling springs seeping from thin fissures, gathering to form streams 1,500 feet below.

The woods open; in the middle of the clearing sits the lodge. Shultis says he built it to be "mouseproof"—there is not one place for a mouse to get in, he insists. I believe him; the place radiates snugness.

The kitchen has a big, black, gas-powered range; in the dining-living area two long tables front a drying rack over a monster wood stove. Behind this big room, a smaller sleeping room accommodates two rows of bunks, and behind that, a wood walkway leads to an outhouse.

Shultis shows me four quadrants of United States Geological Survey maps tacked to the wall. We talk topography, and he tells me of the romps of his younger years.

After closing up the lodge, we return to the jeep and grind down the backside of Hanover, pointing roughly toward the head of Watson Hollow. Shultis wants to check the woods for "shack"—food for game. He spots some large black-cherry trees. "Lumberman's gold," he calls it. Grade-one black cherry brings a dollar per board foot; a mature tree yields about 200 feet.

Shultis forages through the woods as I sit in the jeep taking notes. The shack this year on top of Hanover looks poor—frost hit the oaks in blossom, and there are no acorns. Back at the cabin, I ask if I can walk back down the mountain.

As the jeep growls into the valley and out of hearing, I feel liftings that verge and turn to a soar. I think of Roethke's lines: "We think by feeling. What is there to know?/I hear my being dance from ear to ear."

It is getting on toward evening, and at 2,500 feet on the north side of Hanover at the end of September I can feel the coming frost on my fingers and on the backs of my hands.

It takes me an hour to walk down the mountain. When I finally arrive at the Shultis place, the sun is turning the high ridges to incandescent powder, and shadows are thickening in the draws.

THE LAST FARMERS
OF WOODSTOCK:
MAYNARD KEEFE

"YOU GOT TO KEEP PLANTING," said Maynard Keefe as I was leaving. A mixture of sleet and rain pelted us as we stood out in Keefe's yard. The sheep moped. Clayton's horse despondently bowed his head. The yard and pastures of the farm were covered in a sheet of slush, ice, and turkey-grit snow. Ducks called from the barnyard puddle in which they habitually paddled and preened.

We stood in the rain, and Keefe told me he had recently planted 5,000 spruce trees on the land in Willow which he calls the "flats." Next year, along with his boys, he'll put in 150 new apple trees on the other side of the creek near where we were getting drenched. Come spring, a pasture that had lain fallow for three years would be plowed again.

Keefe harvests his hay in two cuttings, which take place early in the summer when the hay's "got strength in it." He owns his own mower, tetter, manure spreader, tractor, and bailer. Vintage machines, they're not going to win any 4H contests. For bed and feed, Keefe brings in about fifty tons of hay yearly. Last summer, due to drought, he'd only cut once; and this year he had to buy hay.

Keefe's farm sprawls up both sides of the upper Sawkill Valley. Most of the land is now in timber, which he periodically lumbers off. He raises livestock—Holstein heifers sold when they're 2½ years old for $600 to $800, depending on their size, their health, and the quality of their udders.

Dairy farmers buy his heifers for stock. Holsteins, rather than Jerseys or Guernseys, have been in demand because they produce a higher percentage of milk to cream. Keefe's cattle (both "little and big," as he says) this year number twenty-six. When his father was alive, the herd once grew to sixty-eight.

As well as heifers, Keefe has sixty chickens and forty-four sheep. The chickens aren't laying well this time of year; five or six eggs a day is all they produce. We inspect the coop, and Keefe gives me two largish brown eggs.

At Easter, Keefe sells spring lambs for $50 a shot; this year he'll have a crop of about forty-five. The sheep are a problem: "I run the risk of dogs killing them, coyotes catching them," he says, forever the cautious, pessimistic farmer. The previous year he sheared 400 pounds of wool that nobody wanted. In the old days, he sold wool for a dollar a pound, and it was sheared by the buyer to boot.

I ask Keefe if the farm makes money. "Very hardly," he says. Some years, a bit; mostly he breaks about even.

"We've had our best already with the use of the land, you know what I mean." I have to agree.

The Sawkill is a young stream where it races past Keefe's place. The ground around the clapboard farmhouse is wet and full of gullies, puddles, soft spots, and freshets when it rains. Keefe takes a perverse pleasure lamenting this dampness.

The farmhouse has a front porch and a side porch that leads into the kitchen, which is sparse and cool, with linoleum and a couple of long windows. The floors and ceilings of the old house sag. Deer heads are mounted on the walls of the living-dining room. The big eating table is covered with plastic. I spent much of my several interviews with Keefe at this table, while he sat in an overstuffed armchair next to the phone.

Keefe said his grandfather, Johnson, bought 100 acres and a smaller version of the present farmhouse when he moved north from Chesterfield County, Virginia, to Woodstock in 1867. Johnson Keefe and his wife, Jane, grew corn and potatoes and raised cattle. The Keefes are of Scots blood, and after Johnson had died, Maynard's father, Herb, bought the place from his mother, "seeing as no one else wanted a part of it."

Keefe said his father paid for "every teaspoon" of the homestead. "My father was an independent man, didn't want any sympathy from anyone." Herb Keefe kept to farming, adding to his herd, and dabbled in various enterprises on the side. Keefe said Herb sold meat to the area hotels and took his old Model-T Ford up to the top of Overlook to collect the payroll from the Mountain House.

With capital raised through his various endeavors, Keefe's father bought land in great quantity. At his death he owned 1,800 acres in the township, the best part an unbroken swath stretching from Overlook over Hutchin Hill into Mink Hollow and then through Willow. His 1,800 acres made him the largest private landowner in Woodstock.

Keefe said his father "had a habit of not filling his deeds." Keefe gave the impression that the reams of documents and deeds his father left behind are full of hidden pieces of land that no one knows about and secret, mysterious, and complex arrangements that Keefe is still sorting through and puzzling over.

At sixty-eight, Keefe is remarkably sturdy and carries heavy loads without complaint. His hair is more black than gray. Clean-shaven and barrel-chested, he walks with a lumbering, bearish gait. He's friendly, confiding, and elusive by turns and likes to gab. But his most outstanding characteristic are his hands which are large and etched with furrows. They are chartacous, like sheets of parchment that have been crushed and imperfectly smoothed. Cracked and caked, they're always dirty—the dirt worked in, a part of the skin's pigment and texture. Sometimes they look huge, swollen, and bruised. I have a vivid memory of those hands draped over the steering wheel when Keefe used to pick me up in his truck as I hitched around town, too young to drive. They appear as both antithesis and akin to those of a concert pianist's, in that they express a practice unflinchingly pursued, although Keefe's have served no higher purpose than working the land, husbandry, and upkeep of the homestead. They are a living ledger of what it takes to farm the higher regions of the Catskills.

In *The Gift of Good Land*, Wendell Berry writes in an urgent polemic:

> The small farm cannot be 'developed' like a product or a program. Like a household, it is a human organism, and has its origin in both nature and culture. Its justification is not only agricultural, but is part of an ancient pattern of values, ideas, aspirations, attitudes, faiths, knowledges, and skills that propose and support

the sound establishment of people on the land. To defend the small farm is to defend a large part, and the best part, of our cultural inheritance.

Small farms like Keefe's are dying out, not only in Woodstock but all across the country. Agribusiness has taken over with corporate values based on large-scale profits, rather than the small-scale satisfaction of self-sufficiency, independence, and intimacy with the land. In a society that tends to be highly mobile, small farms provide a bulwark of stability, a marriage through generations (like Johnson, Herb, and Maynard Keefe) to place that is immutable. As crucial to Woodstock's character as the vaunted image of itself as an arts colony is an agricultural heritage and the past vitality of its farmers.

That stone walls have become part of real estate advertising borders on the grotesque. I wonder what the farmers who pulled and dredged, blasted and heaved, lugged, hauled, and stacked those walls all over the township would think of the use to which the land is now being put. That kind of back-breaking, unremitting labor, that blind fury of dedication and aspiration toward productivity, deserves something better than to be used as a ploy to boost property values. Woodstock's present zoning law only peripherally addresses the section of the Brown and Anthony Master Plan that identified over 4,000 acres in the township as prime agricultural land.

When Keefe was a child, he walked three miles every day to school. "I grew up with the trees," he said, gesturing toward the wooded mountainsides. When he was a child, they were open fields. The day before Christmas, at the end of my last interview with Keefe, we stood talking in the yard as the freezing rain and sleet pelted down. I thought about Keefe's daily walk to school and the seventeen children born in the farmhouse behind us. Only one died.

Wraiths of mist slipped down the cold back face of Overlook; all around came a steady beat, spit, patter, and hiss. The Sawkill sounded like stones being torn. Keefe quickly shrugged his shoulders, half rolled his eyes, and smiled—a gesture that said plain as words "What are we doing out here in this weather? We must be fools!" He hustled back to the house. Sodden as I turned toward my car. I had the feeling, watching Keefe in his padded red plastic cap and plaid, red wool hunting jacket, that he could stand all day in such weather like a totem pole and not suffer any ill effects.

When I returned home, the first thing I did was fry those two brown eggs. They were delicious, far better than store-bought, as Keefe had promised.

THE ICE PALACE OF KAATERSKILL FALLS

WEST SAUGERTIES

IN MID-WINTER I WENT to photograph the great ice cone that forms under Kaaterskill Falls. Turning onto West Saugerties Road after a late start, I remembered that I had driven this way twenty years before on the back of my uncle's BMW European touring bike. We took off to hit the deep gorges in Palenville when the sun hit the water for a few brief hours summer afternoons.

"Cojones," my uncle said, hefting his jewels like a ball-player before walking off the forty-foot ledge of Fawn's Leap and plummeting into the deep, gravel-bottomed pool. He had a big belly and made a huge splash. I remember water the color of a frog's back and counting: one... and then detonation.

In those days, West Saugerties Road was strictly a no-man's land, its most salient feature the dump, a forbidden and slightly sinister playground where I imagined Clarence Schmidt (like a beautiful but demented Father Christmas) foraging for dolls' heads, fenders, candelabra, Christmas lights, old furniture, broken appliances—scraps he turned into a palace that reflected his obsessive imagination.

When the anarchist flag flew at Holly Cantine's in May, I heard stories about Keitelesque characters who snuck into the dump at night and blasted rats with .22s and searchlights. There were always fires burning, and in my mind's eye scavengers wandered through a Bosch-like landscape of smoldering ruins.

My uncle would cruise at moderate speed past the dump and then downshift into the tall S-turn that begins at Goat Hill Road. I'd lean with him into the curves, and we'd soar toward the mountain, Minister's Face looming close enough to touch. Then he'd really open her up on the long flat. The smooth blacktop shimmered in the heat, and the road was always empty.

We flew past tumble-down farms fronted by fields, wide slate ledges, shallow ground littered with stone scrap. This was rattlesnake country. They slid through the oak woods thick as flies; they slept in wells; they lurked in the boarded-up tar-and-shingle outbuildings we left sagging in our wake.

We made the trip to Palenville often that summer. Heading home, the evening sun would shine in our eyes. I have an image of my uncle sitting on the lawn in front of our house, wearing a white robe, hair pulled back in a pigtail, and a long, bamboo hash pipe with a tiny black bowl in his mouth. He seemed infinitely far away and gloriously lawless.

When I close my eyes before I sleep I have the sensation of falling. The wind curls back my lips and my heart is in my mouth. The emerald water fills the caves of my lungs and I'm amphibious—a fluid coolness slipping into the hollow places.

In my dream, I see two clear teardrops of venom trembling on the tips of hooked fangs.

HUNTERS

Today, West Saugerties is no longer a backwater; developments sprout up everywhere. As I drove, I mourned the demise of snakes which I'd once imagined in every rustling leaf. I passed Raycliff and the Glasel place. Further along, I noticed cars in front of the Ridge Runner Rod and Gun Club. Curious, I stopped.

I knocked on the door and was ushered into the club house, where there were mounted trophy heads, long tables, and an American flag. Half a dozen men were gorging themselves on venison, smoked trout, and beer.

"What the hell do you want?" said one in tones of drunken good humor with something else underneath.

"Do you hunt?"

"Are you packing?"

"Have some meat!"

I found myself with a venison sandwich on a hard roll. The flesh, coated with pepper, was superb: lean, pink in the middle, and tender. When I told them I didn't hunt but did fish, I was presented with a slab of smoked steelhead, which I ripped and gnawed at out of politeness.

I asked to take their photograph. They joshed in earnest, trying to undress, cursing a blue streak, tumbling over each other, and asking me where they should put the whipped cream. Finally, several members of the club (which somewhere along the way I learned was started in 1962, has 200 members, and owns twenty-six acres) settled down and obliged me with a shot. I left them to their own devices, inspected the empty shooting range, and proceeded on my way.

BLUE MOUNTAIN COUNTRY

Blue Mountain sprawls beneath the upthrust prow of

Round Top and High Point Mountains. The land forms a rough triangle between Platteclove and Palenville gorges, the base of the triangle is perhaps ten miles across, the point of which is Tannersville. Dominating this territory are High Peak and Round Top Mountains. Under their shadows, back roads trail off into the sticks—bleak in the February drought, ground frozen solid, pinched into brittle ridges and nubs. Up the escarpment the land turns quickly to state preserve.

Arthur Henry's 1904 memoir *The House in the Woods* gives a clear picture of the interior of this triangle, similar today to what it was a hundred years ago. In the book, Henry recounts moving from New York City to Platteclove, where he built a house and started a small farm. Looking for Utopia, he was soon dispossessed of the notion that rural living is anything but unremitting toil. Here, Henry depicts with characteristic eccentricity, a climb to the top of High Peak Mountain:

> I have never cared to visit High Peak again. One such appalling view of the world is enough for me. I am glad to know that our earth is but an insignificant speck of dust, in measureless spaces of air—because this it is. But for the few years here still left for me, I wish to feel that its land and seas, its gardens, its forests, and its fields, are real; that in the spring the apple-blossoms are rose tinted, and in the fall one may pick up pippins by hunting in the grass; that my neighbors live near me; that there are pies in the pantry, oil in the lamps, wood in the woodshed, and a book open on the table where I had laid it down. All this seems impossible on High Peak.

It is interesting that Henry opts for a kind of pastoral, rather than a romantic or transcendental, ideal. The sublime, typically seen as a mystical communion with nature in its broadest sense, is, for Henry, unbearably lonely. The type of landscape that evoked the sublime was exemplified by writers and painters of the nineteenth century around Platteclove and Kaaterskill Clove. Kaaterskill Falls was the epitome of the sublime to adherents of what historian Roland Van Zandt has called the "cult of the wilderness."

OAKWOOD

Before reaching the falls, I passed through Blue Mountain country and Pinewood, a short strip of settlement wedged into the notch below Platteclove where Henry made his home. For me, Pinewood will always have a backwoods feel. It will always be a place of exile, a place to escape, to lose yourself in the tight-lipped, close-mouthed, mind-your-own-business rural ambience. (Long ago, the headmaster of my school was caught in shady dealings. He moved to Pinewood.)

I idled along Blue Mountain Road, now County Route 35 (a shortcut of which my uncle and I were very proud to have discovered). It soon joined Route 32, a study in strip development catering to the tackiest caricatures of the Catskill experience.

After a mile or so I turned into Palenville, a town of old rooming houses in various states of disrepair. I stopped in front of one old boarding house with peeling paint, a sagging front porch, and dilapidated cabins to the rear. A battered shingle reading "Oakwood" swung in the wind. I knocked on a side door. A middle-aged woman wearing a blue terrycloth robe answered. Cigarette smoke and the sound of a man's cough filled the room to the rear.

"We honeymooned here thirty-seven years ago," said Mrs. Robert Benson. "Twenty years later we came back and bought the place. I guess we bought it with our hearts, not with our heads."

Cold air streamed through the door. Mrs. Benson and her husband both had the flu, so I left and headed up the clove.

TO THE ICE PALACE

The road that follows the Kaaterskill Clove to its summit in Haines Falls has been designated the Rip Van Winkle trail. Although Irving's most famous story has been frequently read as a kind of paean to the Catskills, another reading suggests Irving satirizes the "cult of the wilderness" and lampoons the idea of the romantic sublime. The enchantment Rip experiences is debilitating rather than inspiring—he wakes from his sleep old and feeble. Like Arthur Henry, Rip is eager to return to pies in the pantry and neighbors close at hand.

The state has cut a half-mile trail that branches off the road into the bottom of the Kaaterskill Falls. The trail looked as though it has hosted a stampede. Raw roots snaked over packed ground like arthritic fingers. The day I walked it, the trail was a sheet of ice.

The half mile took me almost an hour. I came out of the woods and stood at the base of the falls. Huge fangs of ice had formed off the lip of the first drop hundreds of feet above. Water rushed through a frozen spigot and sprayed the peak of the ice cone. I could just make out its top from where I was standing.

A man in his late twenties, wearing a purple Patagonia jacket and white Reeboks, was walking gingerly across the top of an ice-covered boulder. He was visiting from Long Island for the day.

"I tried to climb up there," he said, pointing to the fall's top. "Halfway up it got too hairy. I turned around. I nearly killed myself coming down."

I looked at the steep, icy bank with no great enthusiasm. But part of my quest that day was to view the great ice cone in all its glory. I left him eating a Hershey bar and setting up a gleaming aluminum tripod, and started what turned into an arduous and dangerous scramble—grasping at roots, heaving and hauling myself upward body length by body length, relying on frozen footholds and precarious rock outcroppings ready to give way at any time and send me tumbling down into the frozen chasm.

After much distress, I pulled myself level to a narrow path that hugged a sheer rock face encased in ice. The path was frozen solid and slick as a skating rink. I inched my way forward wishing for the hundredth time that I had crampons and a better sense of balance. The trail turned a corner and opened onto a wide rock ledge which commanded a splendid view of the falls and surrounding stone amphitheater. I was perched above the ice cone, which I leisurely perused. Relishing its flatness, I sprawled on the ledge. The view of the cone, I decided (even while trying to convince myself that the way down did not mean certain death) was worth the climb. Fifty feet across at its base, the cone looked like a sarcophagus for a new kind of creature—the palace of an ice worm, its larva gestating in the inner recesses, waiting to fetter the mountains in a millennium's worth of snow.

In his diaries, the nineteenth-century painter Thomas Cole describes the amphitheater and the ice cone: "There are overhanging rocks and dark-browed caverns, but where the spangled cataract fell stands a giant tower of ice, reaching from the basin of the waterfall to the very summit of the crags."

When I was there, the long incisor of ice and the tip of the cone on which the falls spattered had not quite joined. As I sprawled, peaceably revelling, a group was perched on the lip of the falls playing congas and guitar. Four college students, beer cans in hand, ambled around the corner of the path and gave me a nod. They had come down from above. In raucous tones, they began discussing the evening's debauch. Stiffly, I righted myself. The way down turned out not to be so bad. I slid down on my ass, most of the time with a fair degree of control.

At the bottom I was greeted with the most extraordinary sight: There, on the flat rock where I had left the Patagonia-Reebok man, was a younger man, dressed in a coon-skin hat, knickerbockers, galoshes, a turn-of-the-century short wool jacket, and a tie. When I asked him who he was, he laughed and said that he was a transient philosopher. Immediately following were three other men in similar attire. They were lugging a large nineteenth-century polished wooden camera with a wooden tripod. This group turned out to be Messrs. McDermott and McGough, their associate James Wheeler, and young initiate Jeffrey Gasperini, all painters and photographers who use nineteenth-century techniques and subjects. They also live, think, and talk in nineteenth-century style, as I found out later.

"Artists who worked here saw this as a direct link to paradise," said David McDermott, speaking of Hudson River School painters like Thomas Cole and Frank Church who had painted in the Catskills. McDermott was willowy, with a choir-boy's voice and a shock of red hair. "They saw the land as intact from the beginning of time, not like Europe where every gorge had been dug for rock. We're keeping alive the tradition."

We chatted a while, then said adieus. My balance was far improved heading down the trail. There was still a patch of daylight left. I decided to take the long way home. I drove through Tannersville, Stony Clove, Chichester, and Phoenicia.

I thought about those days with my uncle in the gorges above Palenville, which held paradise before my eyes. Alluring and mysterious, it flickered in the emerald water and flew into my mouth when I launched myself from

Fawn's Leap and plummeted downward. It shone in my eyes when I emerged, newly formed, from the hidden recesses of the grotto. Both my uncle and I were mesmerized in very different ways by life's possibilities. After traveling through Europe for years he was looking for something to do, a place to live. He was my present age that summer when he sat smoking hash on our lawn at sunset. Like the transcendentalists, he was looking for ecstasy, the sublime, the discovery of the wilderness within. I tried to remember what I had taken into myself and what I had cast aside. The choices of the past seemed insignificant compared to the choices of the present; but I knew that wasn't so. I followed the Wittenberg Valley back to the center of town.

ON THE NORTH SIDE
OF THE VALLEY

THE GUARDIAN TRAIL

IT'S A MILE AND A HALF UP the Mount Guardian trail, a short hike I take twice a week. The trail twists and turns, threading through laurel, oak, blueberry, and scrub. It loops back on itself, twice crossing a small stream, and skirts an abandoned quarry. At the summit, a large stone cantilevers over the mountainside. I sit there or sprawl, as the mood takes me, and look down on Woodstock.

The white steeple of the Dutch Reform Church is perhaps three miles as the crow flies; Route 212 cleaves through the trees. Little box-like cars cling to its pavement; brave pilots at the helm commandeer their lives. I think about my own life, the car I will get into later that day, the key I will turn. I count the cars just east of the Bearsville Flats. April 19: 4:10 p.m. to 4:11 p.m., eight cars; 5:14 p.m. to 5:15 p.m., ten cars.

I admit, it's a perverse habit—this counting of cars. It's morbid, like a man with a heart condition who's always taking his pulse.

5:35 p.m. to 5:36 p.m., fifteen cars.

My notes from April 19 include the following: Everything has a supernormal clarity/talons hang from a hawk's belly/limbs that snap into strength/like a black belt's fist at the moment of impact/rusty glow on hardwood tips/humps of Wittenberg and Cornell/above the citadel of supporting peaks.

BEARING THE PALL

Looking south and east from the summit, I command a view of the Hudson Valley that stretches from Kingston to Bear Mountain. A pall often hangs over this vista; its color ranges from red to brown to yellow. Is this merely a trick of light or pollution? I called Rob Martin, Principal Engineering Technician, Air Resources Group Department of Environmental Conservation, Region 3.

What I saw was probably refraction from a vapor plume rising off the Hudson, Martin said. Cool water creates a misty film in the warmer air; such plumes can rise to a height of 300 to 400 feet. He added that ozone alerts in the Hudson Valley are caused by unusual heat and fluke atmospheric inversions.

When I asked how he arrived at these benign conclusions, Martin explained the process through which the DEC collects its air data. Nitrogen oxide, lead particles, carbon monoxide, and ozone levels are checked from trailers spaced along the Hudson River and monitored at ground level. Air samples are also collected from riverside utility towers at an altitude of 300 to 400 feet. This information is put together in what Martin called a "convoluted puzzle."

Before getting off the phone, he assured me that what I had witnessed was doubtlessly a natural phenomenon. "People see all kinds of things that scare them but are really quite harmless."

Not satisfied, I called the office of state assemblyman Maurice Hinchey in Albany. Hinchey's staff had no information about air pollution in the Hudson Valley. They suggested I call the DEC in Albany. I spoke to a number of people there and finally connected with Ted Davis, Director of Air Planning. Davis explained that there are two bands of air pollution over the Northeast: The first is ozone pollution that stretches from Virginia to Maine; the second is acid rain which comes from the Ohio Valley and blankets the northern coastal states into Quebec, hitting New York and New England particularly hard. Davis said that what I had seen was probably the belt of pollution that stretches from the capital region to New York City and "tends to slosh up and down the Hudson Valley."

People see things that scare them all the time.

Who would you believe?

LOW-IMPACT MONK

It is Saturday, just before noon. I'm driving down Upper Byrdcliffe Road on my way to the recycling center when I pass a man walking briskly, swinging his arms. He charges aerobically forward in shiny black tights, satin short-shorts, a purple corduroy baseball cap, sunglasses, and a walkman. Under the cap, his face glows. It's drizzling slightly, the temperature in the low fifties.

A woman who is probably his wife, decked out in a bright yellow slicker and sunglasses, huffs along twenty paces behind. She madly swings her arms, futilely pumping her shorter legs to close the gap. But the man was not about to slow for her or anyone; I can tell by his stride and his complete involvement in an experience for which he has carefully orchestrated all the elements. The couple is animated, like a cartoon: the bunny with monocle and top hat wreaking havoc at the opera; the duck stalking through a pastorale cradling a .12-gauge. I visualize the walker back in his weekend home. Invigorated, he peels off the black spandex. His lungs swell with what he doubtlessly thinks is fresh air. To him, country life is a recreational opportunity, a getaway, an escape, the valve that lets the pressure out of the cooker, innocence renewed, sweet dreams when work is done, someplace to sprawl, health, sanity. He jumps into a hot shower. Water pulses over his revitalized body.

The scene at the recycling center is social: Adults stop to chat, and kids tumble down a mountain of newspaper stacked in a forty-foot trailer. I rid myself of thirty pounds of newsprint, fifty gallons of glass, and three dozen plastic bottles. The glass shatters when dumped into metal barrels (for once, that sound does not symbolize for me vandalism and loss). Driving home, I think of the Chinese monk who lives up the road and reuses everything. He writes poems on pieces of brown paper bags. His weekly garbage yield might fill a flowerpot. Each day, when not meditating or drinking cups of tea, he walks a mile for his mail. On the Buddha's birthday, he goes to the city.

Low-impact monk.

April 23: Cool vapor/scrub oaks veiled/big mountains southwest/cloaked in mist

CLOUDY VISION

I'm a purist, I think as sweat cools between my scapulae and I scan the valley after a quick climb. I find living in a chemical bath infuriating. Only a saint wouldn't want to slap the faces of Lawrence G. Rawl and the other Exxon satraps—a $1.1 billion settlement and on with business as usual. Put it into developing renewable energy or conservation programs. Wean the hogs from the trough. Only the brain-dead can listen with complacency to George Bush say that oil exploration must proceed in the Arctic National Wildlife Refuge. Well heads burn in Kuwait. Soot showers the desert.

April 25: 4:14 to 4:15. Nine cars. Vision/clouded/by emotion. Or so the corporate lobbyists say.

Can you imagine the Dorian Gray–like image created by their rhetoric? Can you see the portrait in the attic of the White House?

Several years ago, I first read of the ozone hole moving north toward the pole. I was living in Alaska and used to relish looking from my back porch, thinking that in the 400 miles between me and the Bering Sea there probably wasn't another human being. That was the winter of 1986, the winter of Chernobyl.

UNDILUTED JOY

The Edenic qualities of nature have often been misconstrued. A wolf pack devours the caribou cub while it's still alive. During the last steps of that danse macabre soothing chemicals protect the prey. People who have survived grizzly attacks say that terror turns to dreamlike calm. They felt no pain—a reassuring thought. Predator and prey are bound in a compact of blood. In essence, the whole thrust of consciousness has been to transcend this relationship—to break the cycle. "Enough slaughter," says the low-impact monk who eats low on the food chain.

Spiritual joy has its basis in the sensual. Ask Gerard Manley Hopkins. Religious responses of happiness, ecstasy, and awe derived from prayer, meditation, or mystical communion manifest physiologically. Recently, I have found it increasingly difficult to experience moments of undiluted joy, this prime pleasure of existence which has always been, for me, linked to nature.

Undiluted joy. There is no place on the planet left un-
contaminated, to some degree, by waste pouring into air,
water, and earth. I ask in my darker moments: How is it
possible to walk with eyes open and not be in a constant
state of mourning?

The Environmental Protection Agency announced that
it's "shocked" at the amount of toxic waste that industry
dumps—some twelve million tons yearly (an admittedly
low estimate).

Shocked? The agency empowered to protect our en-
vironment?

We had no idea the problem was so vast, they claim.
Where have they been?

Woodstock should pass an ordinance to put stocks on
the village green. Our judges could use this form of in-
carceration for environmental offenders, from litterers on
up.

April 26. Dusk. *Cars, cars cars!* I race down the Guardian trail—waiting to trip, put weight on the wrong stone.
Hear an ankle snap.

NOON SIRENS

Recently, making my journalistic rounds, I heard that
someone had petitioned the Woodstock Environmental
Commission to do something about the noon siren set
off by the Woodstock firehouse. This fellow said his peace
of mind was being eroded by the siren's daily wail. No
one knew what to make of the request.

Was the siren noise pollution or a time-honored tradition? How would the guys in the firehouse feel if the siren
didn't blow? The Commission agreed that if the man
didn't like sirens he shouldn't have moved behind the
firehouse. No use complaining now.

I called fire chief Mike Densen who said he'd just as

soon do away with the noon siren, an unnecessary equipment test. "Call me back in a couple of days," said Densen. "We'll conduct an experiment. Disconnect it and see if anyone complains." Someone did, and Densen reinstituted the blow.

On top of Guardian, the siren is piercing, ascending, and urgent. It's always with a measure of relief that I realize it's simply noontime, not Armageddon. What follows is usually a mild euphoria floating in the doubly empty hush.

SAMSONVILLE, KRUMVILLE, AND THE COUNTRY BEYOND

NEW MOONS WERE CARVED into the blue shutters of the farmhouse, which was lovingly cared for. The surrounding fields gave the impression that the farm had once straddled Route 3. A car careened around a turn and sped past. I was curious about the history of the place and knocked on the farmhouse door. No one was home, so I turned and walked back to my car through high grass, which was heavy with morning dew.

I had driven here across the Shokan bridge, my mind on a rendezvous. It was a cool night long ago, and we made a pact to meet again on that same bridge sometime in the distant future. I knew her heart wasn't in it. Her lips were as evasive as her eyes; and I felt a thin blade turn, remembering her averted face in the intrusive beacons of the passing cars.

These memories submerged as I entered unknown country, following Route 3 south toward Samsonville. Richard Lionel De Lisser—whose *Picturesque Ulster*, published in 1896, was one of the initial inspirations for this collection—thought of the area as a no-man's land: "Krumville...is the name of another of the small places, or districts, that seem loath to concentrate in any one spot, but prefers to spread itself all over the limit of its boundary." He moves on to the bustle of Shokan, which he found much more to his liking.

A century later, De Lisser would still be piqued by this stubborn diffusion. A back country that is neither mountain nor valley, not the Esopus and not yet Roundout, a southern flank of the Catskills that is orientated toward the backside of the Shawangunks. It is an area of swamps, undulating hills, broad ledges, and limpid streams. The architecture and terrain have been shaped by the farming and stone-house tradition of Hurley, as well as the tanning and mill industries spawned by fast-moving mountain water. But unlike De Lisser, I was to find this ambiguity and diffusion one of the region's principal charms.

Like the rest of the Catskills, however, Samsonville, Krumville, and the country beyond are changing. Further along I stopped to interview some surveyors. A mile or so from where we stood, a new house with a brassy glass front looked down from the gap between Mombaccus and High Point Mountains. The head surveyor, who had crinkly hair pulled back in a pigtail and a machete strapped to his hip, unrolled a map: Dove Hills, sixteen parcels with an average lot size of 3.5 acres. We chatted. Business was booming, he said; subdivisions planned all over the county. I asked him how much the Dove Hill lots were going for. That ended the exchange.

Later I passed through the tiny center of Samsonville: a white Methodist church across from a one-room schoolhouse, a couple of low fences, a dip, and a sharp turn in the road over a bridge that spans the Mettacahants. I dropped in on Jim Burggraf who'd been collecting archeological artifacts from upstate sites for fifty years. In his late seventies, Burggraf was lank and a bit deaf and had foggy glasses and hands that looked like they were once capable. He lives alone in a big house by Samsonville Falls. Burggraf is a rich repository of information. Once he'd warmed up, he talked a blue streak for well over an hour while we poked around his private museum, an impressive jumble of whaling memorabilia and Indian artifacts from sites in the Hurley area. I viewed pestles used for grinding acorns, which were pulverized, roasted, and soaked in water to get the tannin out before being turned into cakes. Burggraf said the Hurley sites are from the 2,000 to 3,000 B.C. range.

Burggraf exhibited flint javelin points taken from two Samsonville rock shelters. Spears were used with throwers to extend their length. Burggraf knew only two shelter sites in Samsonville, but was sure there must be more. As he said this, an intensity surfaced. The passion of a lifetime flaring up, an abiding curiosity rekindled.

We closed up the museum and went to view the wide thirty-foot falls. "Running good," Burggraf said, pleased to have me view it in its glory. He pointed to pilings across the stream, where a grist mill once operated, and explained (amused by my ignorance) that grist is corn, wheat, barley—any pulverized grain. The largest tannery in the country once operated nearby, as did a sawmill.

We talked fishing. Burggraf reminisced about a twenty-three–inch brookie he had caught in 1940 a couple of turns upstream from where we stood, in the faint spray by a rocky pool under Samsonville Falls on the Mettacahants.

I said goodbye, extricating myself from what had become Burggraf's rambling monologue on local history, archeology, and garrulous observations on the decline of the West. As I was leaving, Burggraf mentioned he had yet to catalogue much of the Hurley material, admitting he hadn't had the energy. The hot noon sun beat down. It was a sad, awkward moment. In his proud way he was asking for help. I thanked him for his time and apologized for the disruption. Then I drove away.

Kevin and Linda—new friends who introduced me to the Samsonville area—live further down the Mettacahants on Dewitt Road. Several years earlier they'd bought their little cabin, which was cozy and very country, without plumbing or a well. They come up regularly from the city for long weekends.

Kevin had started fishing Catskill waters three years before and quickly became obsessed. Now he is a "walking advertisement" (as he puts it) for Orvis products. To see him decked out in his fishing regalia—stalking upstream through a still pool with the stealth and patience of a panther for a shot at an eight-inch trout—is to realize one is in the presence of a grand passion. Kevin's bible is *Catskill Rivers* by Austin M. Francis. The book is an engrossing survey of Catskill history and topography, hydrology, and entomology and is filled with fishing lore and practical angling advice. In his introductory essay, "The Catskill Angling Mystique," Francis writes: "Catskill trout streams have a way of leading the fly fisherman through and beyond the conventional stages of angling development from catching the most fish, to the biggest fish, to the most difficult fish, and finally to the soul of the stream."

In this essay and others, Austin talks about the fully "evolved" fisherman—the fisherman who fishes not to catch fish but to practice an art, to reenact with slight variation a Masonic rite, to merge with nature and experience that serenely ecstatic, timeless place. The flowing stream and the rising fish become metaphors, then delicate, but extremely powerful, prompts. My idea of the fully evolved fisherman (if this doesn't sound too preciously Zen) is the fisherman who rarely if ever fishes and, when he does, seeks first to understand the wellspring of his desire. As in all supra-refinements of animal passions,

I wonder if this is the root of civilization or just its facade. Perhaps they are one and the same. At any rate, when Kevin fished, I was mostly content to loll about watching him and turning over the metaphysics of angling in my mind.

That afternoon, blazing hot as it was, Kevin dissuaded me (without difficulty) from clambering up High Point as I had planned. Instead, we took a long journey down through Cherrytown, Lackawack, and around the Roundout in search of undiscovered Catskill fishing waters—which we once again failed to find. On a dry fly just east of Grahamsville I caught a small brookie. But I was more taken with the huge rhododendrons that seemed to grow wild by the streamside than with the fishing. I spent most of my time wallowing nude behind a boulder in a swirling eddy while Kevin assiduously worked the undercuts of shady banks without effect.

Cherrytown was an interesting combination of tacky resorts, gorgeous old farms, dirt-poor farms, new subdivisions, redneck stockcars, and ethnic retreats. We stopped at Rov Tov Satmar, an orthodox Jewish camp where everyone was in flutter before Shabbat and no one had time to talk. There was Hebrew script on all the signs and a barracks-like atmosphere. "Come back Monday! Come back Monday, and I'll be happy to tell you everything you want to know," said a man before plunging back to frantically slicing rye bread.

Back in Samsonville, evening was in the air. We swam in the Mettacahants running full and cool. High Point and an urge for an overview of the region still nagged at me. So, cool, relaxed, and spent though I was, Linda and I hopped in the car and drove up Freeman Avery Road for a walk on the old Kanape Trail that heads over the gap between Mombaccus and High Point Mountains into the head of Watson Hollow. Freeman Avery Road abruptly ended at a chain; large signs that said "no trespassing" and "road closed" were liberally and strategically placed. No sooner were we out of the car than a man was pounding up the road with his hands in his pockets and a bent, determined air.

E. McCully was his name, and he has most emphatically closed the old Kanape Trail. McCully owns a fair chunk of Mombaccus Mountain, which it seems he bought piecemeal over the years. He said he closed the trail because of all the "snowmobiles, ATV's, and every other goddamned thing." His edict also encompasses hikers, and no way was he going to let us mosey up his ¾-mile road to state land.

"Closed tight as a drum," Linda said.

We drove part of the way down the road and followed an old logging trail up the mountainside through open woods. A sinewy stream slammed down a steep gulch as I put my thighs in high gear for what I determined was going to be the last major effort of the day.

A thousand yards up, I forded the stream and broke into freshly cleared open land. A slim man was absorbed in digging a shallow ditch around his house. He had salt-and-pepper hair and wore nothing but black Calvin Klein underwear, black nylon socks, and Reeboks. The house was the very one I had seen earlier, with brassy glass and commanding views. The half-naked digger gave me permission to look around and take some photos. Walking back down his long, precipitous driveway I was in a muck sweat. At its bottom, I dunked my head in the rushing stream. The water tasted and smelled of earth and roots, but its deepest flavor and feel was of gray rocks, the mountain's core, a primo Catskill draught. I stood there dripping, exhausted, and happy as a dog.

It was dusk and dinnertime. We picked up Kevin and headed off to the Krumville Country Inn, which is perched above a beautiful swamp and filled with interesting knickknacks (including a hundred-pound stuffed tarpon). But its most outstanding feature is the 200 kinds of beer served, all catalogued and priced on colorful wooden-slat signs. Talk about decisions! Kevin ordered Dragon Stout, a thick, sweet, frothy brew bottled in Kingston, Jamaica. I let Linda choose for me. She chose Weiss Spatan, a dry beer served with a wedge of lemon run around the rim of the glass.

I remembered this beer from my trip to Munich the previous December. A bitter wind blew snow from the east. That night, I ate spetzal and drank beer in a bar where, through a glass wall, affluent young Bavarians watched a white stallion gallop around an indoor pavillion. A ringmaster in tight shiny britches brandished a whip and guided the horse through its paces. The sense of contained power was mesmerizing, the scene a bit perverse.

That night, eight months later, Kevin, Linda, and I dined on just passable but cheap fish and chips. When we walked outside it was close to 10 p.m. and still warm. Our steps crunched in the gravel lot. I heard water falling on stone and the insect trill, like tiny tambourines and castanets. The waning gibbous moon, tremendous and yellow, lorded over Krumville.

I retraced my route, passing Dove Hills and the blue-shuttered farmhouse, whose windows were dark. I stopped on the reservoir bridge and got out of the car, transfixed by the dancing path the moon laid down on the water, looking like the road to Oz. Small waves lapped against rocks at my feet, and the wind smelled of deep water. I waited and waited. Then I drove home with all the windows open, night air thrashing through the car.

TO ECHO LAKE
AND BACK

THERE ARE MANY WAYS to approach Echo Lake: You can ford Platteclove and dip down between Overlook and Plattekill Mountains, or you can approach the lake from basically the same orientation but further up the range, say coming in from Elka Park to Pecoy Notch and then hiking the jagged ridge of Indian Head Mountain before casting off one of its southern spurs and trying to hit the lake by compass or dead reckoning.

In mid-November, I hiked a circular route to Echo Lake and back, starting at the parking lot on top of Meads Mountain and following state trails. From the lake, I bushwhacked along the Sawkill's headwater into Keefe Hollow, then climbed back to MacDaniel Road.

Climbing Overlook I've always been curious about the many paths branching off the main trail. As I puffed along they seemed full of promise—shortcuts that follow the contours of the Sawkill Valley instead of circuitously climbing to the top of Overlook before dropping roundabout to the lake.

I cast off the trail and merrily followed a series of fading white blazes. It looked like a promising shortcut. Soon, however, the old road turned completely in the wrong direction and became a spring-filled morass. I thrashed about in a tangle of fallen limbs and skewed boulders, vainly trying to cut back to state trail. Finally I gave up in disgust and retraced my steps. Upwards I trudged, stopping to eat cheese and crackers where the trail splits above the ruins of the old Overlook Mountain House. Next to its blasted hulk, the WTZA-TV tower hummed ominously.

My body cooled, and I drank some water. The wind sounded torrential but far away; clouds shot from the north, torn and insubstantial. I lounged on a wilted filigree of November grass. Rustling goldenrod shivered in a faint breeze, and the sun was strong. Hefting myself, I started down the road which once connected the Mountain House to Platteclove, Tannersville, and eventually the Catskill Mountain House.

Roland Van Zandt, in his book *The Catskill Mountain House,* argues that in the early nineteenth century, Americans were still swayed by the aesthetic doctrine of "Association" (imported from Europe) which "defined an ideal landscape in terms of its rich association with ruins and relics, myths and legends." Van Zandt goes on to assert that American Romanticism liberated itself and its vast creative power by divining a transcendent order in the wilderness—a landscape unfettered by human history. I wondered if now, over a century later, the ruins of the old hotels and overgrown paths to promontories, once redolent with romance, could be the basis for an American doctrine of association, albeit on a less Jovian scale.

The trail was good walking. I was moving so fast that I almost missed two porcupines perched in a small hemlock. They cast baleful, suspicious glances in my direction, bristling their quills. They gripped the tree trunk, their long claws kneading and retracting. One of the porcupines was big—big as a piglet. The other was small and round and lethargically cowered. Judy Ford, a wildlife biologist, said porcupines climb trees to eat the cambium layer of wood directly beneath the bark that carries nutrients up and down the trunk. Porcupines do well on just this diet. These two porcupines "could have been a family unit, although the mothers don't tend to be real affectionate," Ford said.

Echo Lake is cradled in the lap of Overlook, Plattekill, and Indian Head Mountains on the Ulster-Greene County line. It's one of the few high-elevation Catskill lakes— Balsam, North, and South Lakes are others that come to mind.

Indians frequented the area as late as the middle of the last century according to Arthur MacDaniel, whose family once owned much of the acreage I'd just walked. He said that his grandmother, Sarah Louise, rented boats in the nineteenth century when the lake was a prime tourist attraction. She lived in a house on the lake's north shore with two cows, a dog, the Indians, and tourists for company. MacDaniel said his grandfather was mostly away, tending the family farm, and implied that Sarah Louise took full advantage of her independence. The lake was formed when the glaciers retreated at the end of the last ice age. The soil conservation map identifies the soils around the lake as glacial deposition. The topsoil is shallow and rocky, with tough but friable subsoils to a depth of sixty inches.

Dick Rommel, a forester, said the forest in the area is "transitional"; such forests grow up after land has been cleared. Pioneering species establish themselves, then a transitional forest evolves—in this case, predominantly hardwoods, such as beech, maple, oak, birch, hemlock, and cherry. Rommel said that the oddly circular configuration of the trees around the lake is probably due to silt and soils building in concentric circles around the lake shore as the glacier retreated. The trees take hold where the soil is richest.

Ron Pierce, senior aquatic biologist with the DEC, who surveyed the lake in 1986, said that it's eighteen feet at its deepest point. Most of the bottom is thick muck, and in 1986 it covered thirteen acres. Pierce said he netted brook trout, black and yellow bullheads, and golden shiners during the survey. Two species of bullhead were abundant, as were the shiners; the nets yielded just three brook trout—a yearling of eight inches and a pair of three-year-olds, thirteen and sixteen inches. The low trout count, Pierce thought, was due to pressure from the other species. The state stopped stocking the lake (by helicopter) in the 1970s because, Pierce said, he found clouds of fingerling brookies in the shallows.

Pierce also said that in early June of '86 he did a pH count of lake water which read 6.3 (7 being normal). The pH is affected by acid rain: a lower pH translates into more acidity in the rain- and snowfall. Pierce said he would bet that earlier in the spring, after snow had melted, the pH in the lake would be in the range of 5.

In 1987, Walt Kretser, with the DEC, helped survey a large number of ponds in the Catskills and Adirondacks. The survey has yet to be released by the DEC and so remains confidential. But Kretser did say they found a pH close to 6 at Echo Lake. Kretser characterized the count as "not great but not bad. Not critical."

Yet.

When I visited the lake, there were large numbers of fingerlings in the shallows. It was cool and breezy, and no fish rose. I sat on the lip of the lean-to, garbage from careless campers strewn liberally about, and talked to a professional hiker-type in his late thirties who lived north of Catskill. He wore quilted ski pants and expensive boots. I felt shabby in my ratty long-underwear top and a wool jacket missing all its buttons.

"Just had to get out today. Took off from work. Damn city people," he said, scanning the garbage. "They just trash the place." I gave him some of my yogurt-covered almonds. He looked at my boots, beaten and ragged. "Looks like they've seen some miles."

I said that I'd bought them in the Indian Himalayas, used, the year before and that they looked pretty much the same then.

"I'm afraid when I go to those big mountains the Catskills will be ruined for me," he said. I told him not to worry and went to sit by the lake's shore, to watch the sunlight play on the water and to listen to the wind.

A man and woman came by with four small, thin, and nervous dogs wearing sweaters. The woman kept whistling and beckoning to them, and they would flock to her and then scatter. Ringmaster and sled driver, she called after them as she scampered with her companion around the shore and into the trees.

I sat for a while at the lake's outlet, which is the Sawkill's source. It's strange to see a stream in the Catskills so wide and full at such a high elevation, but the Sawkill flows out of Echo Lake as a full-blown stream, replete with small falls, deep pools, and what looks like good fishing. The outlet is flanked by a primeval hemlock swamp, the trees dense and stunted with roots underwater. I picked my way through this terrain and followed the plunging Sawkill—rough going over deadfalls and slippery rocks.

Scanning my maps I'd noted a clearly marked logging road running parallel to the stream. Half a mile and half an hour later, I discovered a road shadowing the stream, but it soon petered out. The country was very quiet and very clean. Occasionally, I came upon a circle of stones.

Through the trees, the valley curved west and ridges formed steep vees, bisecting each other. Behind me Indian Head reared.

I knew I was in Keefe Hollow.

I came to a pine wood, crossed the stream, and found a good road which led to the foundations of the glass-works village that once thrived behind Keefe's place. Slipping under his gates, I found his wife, Shirley, out in the barn with a grandchild, tending the chickens and cattle. Shirley and I talked about our families and the livestock and waited for Maynard to come down off the hill from cutting wood. It was late afternoon, but the sun was still strong.

Keefe appeared, the back of his truck loaded with wood. We stood on either side of a gate and shot the breeze while Shirley pulled laundry off the line.

The sun was getting low. It dampened in the hollow, and Keefe had his wood to get in. He gave me directions through his pasture to MacDaniel Road: follow the stone wall until you come to a gate; go into the woods and keep the last of the light on your right shoulder. I did just that, moving fast through tangled saplings and scruffy underbrush, my breath vapor in the dusk. I hastened through a hemlock forest recently lumbered and jumped a small stream. Ten minutes after leaving Keefe, I broke out of the trees high on MacDaniel Road just below Magic Meadow.

THE OSTRANDER
PLACE

THE BROCKWAY CLASS-8 dump truck idles beside the shop. It can legally carry a gross weight of 52,000 pounds. Al Ostrander is pushing that limit. The dump-body is packed with long lengths of maple, oak, and ash from Olderbark Mountain off a tract that Ostrander and his father cut thirty years before. Now Ostrander's son Danny works the woods.

The family settled in the Hudson Valley seven generations ago. It shows in Ostrander's speech. He drawls with a nasal twang as though balancing a raw egg yolk on his tongue. Stooped, with thinning hair, his pale, moon face is often lit with a bucktoothed smile. His diffident manner partially conceals a mordant sense of humor and an opinionated nature.

At fifty-eight, Ostrander says he's beginning to slow. That's not surprising considering the fourteen-hour workdays he's put behind him since he could say the word "father." Ostrander grew up as a dairyman's son, working four a.m. to six p.m. six days a week and ten hours on Sunday.

In 1944 his father, Harry, bought the Mosher farm at the head of the Willow Valley. He eventually added the Hasbrouck farm, creating a spread of more than 800 acres. Seven hundred seventy-five acres remain, making it one of the single largest holdings in Woodstock. In 1956, the last herd of sixty cattle grazed 100 acres of fields. Open to this day, they surround the white clapboard fourteen-room farmhouse where Anna May, Ostrander's mother, who is now in her eighties, still lives. Harry died in 1985.

Ostrander has been married twice. The most recent marriage, short-lived, ended badly. His first wife gave him a son and three daughters and died ten years ago in an auto accident on MacDaniel Road. He says he's learned he'll never replace her, implying that it was foolish to have even tried.

After chatting briefly in the shop, cluttered with chain saws in various states of disrepair, we walk out to the idling truck. I scramble up to what seems the impossibly high door of its cab. Ostrander throws the big diesel in gear, and we head over the small rise which only partially obscures the farm's panoramic views. It is a quick half mile down Ostrander Road to Route 212 and the Willow Church.

Ostrander is quiet while driving to Livingston Manor. When we talk it is mostly about the truck or the Woodstock Planning Board on which he is serving. A controversy has his ire up: The board has been trying to decide whether to allow a local developer to sell antiques from his art gallery. This has led to a seemingly endless debate over "what is art?" Ostrander is not in the least amused. "What a waste of time!" he scoffs. The meeting the night before ran past one a.m.

Rain taps intermittently against the truck's soiled windshield. For the longest while Ostrander pays it no mind. Finally he turns on the wipers as we head west through Big Indian. The heavy truck strains cresting Pine Hill. As we drift down into Delaware County, Ostrander lights a Marlboro. Past Margaretville we swing south along the Pepacton's edge and stop just past the bridge that bisects the reservoir. Ostrander checks the load.

"Ever lost one?" I call as he tugs at the chains, pokes the big tires with his boot, and ducks beneath the bed for a quick look at the chassis.

"Not yet," he drawls.

Climbing the long grade up Cat Hollow, he flicks on the blinkers and hugs the shoulder to let cars pass. We chug through Roscoe and follow the Willomec River upstream to Livingston Manor.

The town is full of quaint shops: Razzberries, Shardalee, and Brenda Love, Hat Designer. Along Main Street, a fire has gutted a two-story wooden building. Trucks pump water from the creek to douse the charred remains. An older man in a red slicker conducts traffic and chomps a dead pipe while townsfolk rub elbows. A volunteer fireman of long standing, Ostrander offers "looks like a bad one" and leaves it at that.

The Rocky Vitali Mill, a father-son operation, has its back to the river. The mill used to float the lumber downstream, but it's now carted away by truck. Mountains of unhewn logs are sorted, stacked, and dispatched to the saws by a small troop of yellow Pettibone Carrylifts. The sawbelt's drumming is incessant, pitched suddenly urgent as blades screech, devouring wood. The blades drown out the Pettibone's sputter and hack.

The mill crew curb their language and can the ethnic jokes when Ostrander introduces me as a reporter from Woodstock. They respond to the town's name as though it were a resort on the Black Sea. Rocky, Jr., a clean-cut, bright-faced thirty-year-old, looks like he'd be more at home preparing briefs than grading Ostrander's timber. His job is to measure the diameter of each log and check its length for imperfections. His low shoes are miraculously unsoiled by the muddy chaos of the yard.

Rocky, Jr., hands Ostrander a slip of paper, and we walk over to the mill office. Compared to its surroundings, the office is a haven. Mozart wafts through the room. Alice, an attractive, middle-aged woman, presides. She chides Ostrander as she translates Rocky, Jr.'s figures into cash.

"You're one of my favorite people. A gentleman for sure," she says during their banter. Ostrander chuckles.

Alice needs a ride down the road, and Ostrander, deprecating the comfort of the Brockway's cab, offers her a seat. "I guess I've ridden in worse," she says.

The elder Vitali enters and swiftly appropriates the privilege of conveying Alice. She cuts Ostrander a check which he folds and stashes in the breast pocket of his overshirt. To the invoice he gives not a glance.

"Have a happy!" he says with a half wave, showing his two front teeth.

"See you next week!" says Alice.

"God willing," and we are out the door, business concluded, the mill quiet in the lunch hour, small rain wrung from the sky's gray sheet.

The empty truck is springier, and we bounce out of town. Ostrander asks if I want lunch; we decide to stop at his usual spot in Margaretville, an hour and a half away, and I settle in for the long ride.

We are in the Catskills's southeastern tier, where poverty is commonplace. Trailers spew the contents of marginal lives by the roadside. A madonna statuette beckons with open arms. A mangy hound bucks against a chained spike. Wrecks rust by black-tar pillboxes that sag under the weight of seasons.

We sink into silence, immured in the engine's steady

roar and the unfurling ribbon of the road that wraps and rewraps the passing scene. East of Margaretville, Ostrander pulls the Brockway onto the shoulder and lets the motor idle to cool before shutting down. We cross Route 28 and enter the tavern: a dark room, mostly bar, with one small table, an L-shaped counter, a whirling fan, country music on the jukebox, a Triple Strike Puck Bowl, and buck trophies mounted on the walls.

"Let's see how we made out."

We perch ourselves on counter stools, and Ostrander unfolds the invoice. The load was larger than expected— 2,893 board feet. But because cheap hard maple predominated and there were no veneer quality trees, it grosses only $895.17.

I ask Ostrander how he manages to make money. He replies that if the load had been oak and ash he could "readily have made twice the dollars for the same amount of wood. Logging's no high buck operation. You're not bringing your money to the bank in a wheelbarrow. It's not a monetary richness, but a way of life."

The waitress takes our order: for Ostrander soup, a western omelette, a sandwich, and coffee. "I like my soup," he says. For me, a burger and a Coke.

Logging brings in half Ostrander's income. Another thirty-five percent comes from excavating. He and Danny dig foundations, put in driveways and septic systems, clear land for building sites, and do heavy landscaping. The chain saws account for the remaining fifteen percent.

Danny works on salary, "the same way I worked for my Dad," Ostrander says. He reminisces about the meat-packing house his father owned on the corner of Route 375 and Maverick Road when he was "just a little shaver."

"We ought to be peddling along," he says and insists on picking up the check.

"Next time," I say as we exit.

Ostrander ducks his head and gives me a sidelong look. "Glad to have you along," he replies.

Back in Woodstock, it is close to three. We pass Ostrander Road and the Willow Church. The day isn't over. Ostrander is taking the tops of the trees just delivered to a Boiceville mill. Not nearly as valuable as the thicker trunks, the second load will bring a scant $300.

The logging site is down a rough work road and over a small gully through which crystalline water flows. Timber is stacked everywhere. Ostrander pulls the empty truck in front of a small mountain of logs. He hoists himself into the dump-body, scooping and draping forty-pound lengths of chain over his arm then tossing them to the ground. He jumps from the open gate—a five-foot drop—and lands lightly. Hustling around the body's exterior he lays out the chains, which he'll crane-lift over the full hold "to save back work," he explains almost sheepishly.

Behind the stacked logs sits a 1951 Mack truck on hydraulic stabilizer outriggers with a John Deere Knuckle Boom Picker mounted backways off its bed. The contraption looks rusty, precarious, and makeshift. Ostrander fiddles with the truck's engine which soon putters to life; exhaust foaming through the air. He climbs into the open cab perched above the claw. Working the levers, he spins, pitching logs into the dump-body, then stacking them in the bed. The big metal claw slams the dumper's hull.

Work proceeds apace. Ostrander has the truck full in forty minutes. As he is finishing, Danny approaches from the woods. I go to meet him. We chat and saunter back to where Ostrander is battening down the load.

"How'd we make out?" Danny asks. His nasal whine is similar to his father's, though higher pitched.

Ostrander fishes the invoice from his pocket. They discuss it, smoke and kibitz.

"Get any of your other work done?" says Ostrander in what seems to me a potentially lethal combination of parent and boss. "Noooooo. The way that slab was going and that..."

Danny's a rangy, blond thirty-two-year-old, already touched by Ostrander's stoop. He cuts trees and "skids" them down the mountain—work that used to be done with horses and sleds and is now accomplished with a skidder. The skidder is similar to the Pettibone, a meshed cab mounted like a top hat on four huge wheels. The levitating front fork has been replaced with a winch that funnels tentacles of chain. Danny can singlehandedly fell and trim sixty-foot trees, loop chain around their trunks, winch the lengths into a skein, and skid the whole caboodle behind him down slopes that make expert ski runs look tame.

Ostrander finishes securing the load, I jump into the cab, and we are off on the final voyage of the day. The ride to Boiceville Lumber is a quick jaunt compared to the morning's journey.

After dumping the logs we pass Valerie, the mill's owner, striding across the yard. Ostrander stops, and there is a brief exchange. Young and incongruous amid the stacked lumber and prefab sheds, she took over the operation when her father died. Ostrander's admiration has a wait-and-see edge as he praises her fortitude and perseverance.

Back at the farm we talk for a few minutes before I leave. I'm tired and a little bit numb; Ostrander, on the other hand, looks pretty much the same as he did eight hours earlier. He doles out his energy like his words, always plenty in reserve.

I sit in my small car, dwarfed from riding in the truck all day. It feels clean and safe and civilized. Letting the engine idle briefly before driving off, I close my eyes. I see the falling line of the Willomec as I saw it earlier that day, perched high in the husky's cab. Tendons of water ripple and flex. We speed against the current. Deep in my jaw an engine growls.

Back at the farm a week later, I interrupt Ostrander blowtorching rivets off the top piece of his dozer's scoop. The blade-like, stainless-steel strips that run the scoop's length have been ground to a nub and need replacing. Ostrander puts the task aside to take me to where Danny is cutting on another part of the property.

"Ever ride one of these?" he asks, kick-starting two Suzuki four-wheel, all-terrain vehicles.

"No," I admit.

After Ostrander shows me how to work the gears, I orbit the shop a few times getting the feisty four-wheeler's feel. Ostrander pulls out in front of me, and we go tooling past the farmhouse, the empty chicken coop, hog pen, and snowmobile graveyard (six out of twenty work) into the woods. Almost immediately we are climbing, heading roughly east into Mink Hollow.

Ostrander surges ahead, and I follow as best I can, trying to keep the hand throttle steady as the Suzuki bumps, swoops, and pitches over the rocky logging road. The grade is mostly steep, and there is one hairy moment when Ostrander stalls (he's given me the less troublesome machine), and I have to clutch in, brake, and putter in place while he tries to restart. After several false tries the engine fires and he's off. Releasing the clutch, I stall. Ostrander, looking over his shoulder, waits while I sweat my way out of the jam.

To my relief we soon reach flatter ground. The scruffy woods give way to what obviously was once pasture. Ascending plateaus are dotted with small pines and birch widely spaced in grass, moss, and ferns. Danny has made a hunting camp by slinging a blue tarp across a foundation on what was once the Hasbrouck farm.

Soon the road becomes too rough to ride, so we dismount to proceed on foot. Ostrander praises my driving and explains that his four-wheel is geared higher than mine, which is why he outdistanced me on the hills. A less considerate man would have let it pass. With purposeful ease he moves ahead of me through the woods, holding branches so they won't snap back. After five minutes we hear Danny's saw wail.

Danny is cutting on a flat. Several sixty-foot stripped trunks are already amassed at the skidder's rear. Although we are only 2,200 feet up on Olderbark's side, the 3,300-foot summit looks deceptively close. "You'd be sweating by the time you got up there," Ostrander remarks. We are near the border of the Catskill Forest Preserve and I ask Ostrander if he's ever been approached by the state to sell his land.

"Not yet," he says. "But they pretty much know how I feel."

"How's that?" I ask, unprepared for his vehemence.

Ostrander says that state land is wasted land. Lumbering is akin to agriculture, another form of renewable crop on a longer cycle. He adds that state forest is bereft of game and rejects what he sees as a misguided environmental philosophy. "Take any developed land in the Northeast, turn it over and you'd have a woodland a hundred years later. Development is not some irreversible spoilage process. What a fight it is to keep open fields!"

I stay with Danny who is busy at work and camera-shy. Ostrander walks back to the Suzuki. He offers to pick up my "vehicle" later if I want to ride back to the farm with Danny. I confess that I'm looking forward to driving the four-wheeler back. He's pleased.

Sawdust explodes like fireworks as Danny's racing chain melts wood. He wears goggles, ear-muffs, a hard hat, and kneepads. He drops trees casually, on a dime. Like Ostrander, he works quickly but without apparent haste, handling the bucking saw with ease. A mature maple is felled, trimmed, and winched to the back of the skidder in five to ten minutes.

A spring burbles from the splayed roots of a birch; Danny lowers himself, lapping the pristine water, and I follow suit. We gab briefly about his end of the operation, but he's obviously anxious to keep moving. Soon a full load of trunks is chained to the skidder's rear like a stripped bouquet. He pops into the cab, and the skidder lurches forward. I scramble in the wake of heavy logs mashing against each other, wrenching their chains. At the first steep downhill, Danny stops and I clamber aboard, crouching in a nest of axes, chain saws, and crowbars. Danny pilots the skidder down what seems to me a near vertical grade, wood tonnage churning and smashing behind.

"Isn't this dangerous?" I shout over the engine's roar. Danny gives me a blank look. I try again. "Aren't you afraid the logs will break loose and come through the back of the cab?"

"Sure," Danny says after a pause. "But you got to figure you got it covered."

I hop off at the grade's bottom and with Danny's directions walk uphill to find the Suzuki. Ostrander had turned it around, a task I was anticipating with some apprehension. Again, I'm touched by his courtesy, which is evinced at every turn. It seems as much a part of him as his laconic drawl, the blue oil-stained work jumper with "Al" stitched over the breast pocket, and his dogged provincialism.

Before journeying back, I lean against the Suzuki's side and listen to the faint whisper of the afternoon breeze stirring the forest. I can just hear the skidder's whine far below, like a pebble dropped into a well. I kick-start the small engine. The mellow afternoon detonates as I toe the four-wheeler into gear and head back to the farm.

I spend the better part of the afternoon interviewing Ostrander in the coolness of his shop. The radio is tuned to WRWD, a country-music station out of Highland. I take notes sitting on narrow wood steps going up to a loft. Ostrander sits in a swivel chair at the gun-metal desk where he keeps accounts. The surface is a whirlwind of tattered papers and mechanical doodads. Wasps swing in and out the open door.

When I ask for an inventory of his vehicles and equipment, Ostrander sighs. Looking heavenward he rakes his thin hair. "I'd prefer not," he says. When the conversation lags I go back to the list. It ends up filling four pages in my notebook, the star item a 1937 tractor ("never had the engine apart yet").

We trade fishing stories and talk about how to raise tasty veal calves, how to make good hay, and the road that once ran from Silver Hollow to Chichester and another that ran to Devil's Tombstone. Ostrander gauges that from the end of Silver Hollow and the old farm it is three to four miles to Phoenicia, five or six to Hunter, ten or eleven to Woodstock, and three and one-half miles to the Willow Store.

We discuss the future of the Ostrander place. With characteristic modesty he says "It's just basic Catskill land. Lifts and flats." That description doesn't begin to convey the spectacular views, high rolling fields, and secluded woodland. I ask Ostrander if he is concerned that his heirs might have to break up the holding and sell it off to pay estate taxes, and whether he's considered placing a conservation easement on at least part of the land.

He explains that because of the family's logging operations all his woodland (approximately 675 acres) is enrolled in the Fischer Forest Tax Law and assessed at only twenty percent of its value. In exchange, a six percent stumpage fee is paid to the town in lieu of taxes. The result is that the property's assessed at just under $600,000, which Ostrander says places it within the limits of tax-free inheritance.

Moreover, Ostrander says, "It's not within my prerogative or power to designate how land will be used down the road. No one person has the right to usurp those choices. We *own* land in quotation marks. I feel we just rent it for a while from the Good Lord."

By this time I have writer's cramp and I'm squirming on my slat. I suggest that we tour the barn, which contains shops, livestock stalls, haylofts, and multiple storage areas. A former stable houses an antique, horse-drawn backboard buggy in good condition (it looks like it is ready for a spin) parked beside a pile of tires.

The original section of the barn is cavernous and melodic: rafters, beams, a raised loft, porthole end windows, dusky light, hay odor, and a swayback roof that's provided shelter for nearly two centuries. It's a place for a tryst. Most of the floor is awash with what looks to me like junk. I realize that Ostrander's a pack rat—a predilection which I suspect goes back more than one generation.

Dana LaBarr is the Ostrander daughter who tends to much of the barn work. She and her husband Tom are busy spreading manure on the fields. Two of Ostrander's three daughters have bought small parcels from Anna May and live on the farm. Dana is tallish and wavy-haired with a wide cowgirl stance. Their elfin daughter Dani prances through a skittish slew of cats, horses that nod in their stalls, and a jumble of halters, saddles, reins, rakes, and shovels.

Watching Tom fill the spreader from a large pile of manure by the barn door, Ostrander says: "That's a lesson. A pile of shit don't stink till you stir it up."

Before I leave I ask Ostrander if I can come back once more to interview his mother. "I don't see a problem with that," he replies.

The afternoon has cooled into evening. Danny has gone to a party in town. Anna May, as far as I can tell, has kept to the house all day. Dana and Tom work the barn and fields in tandem. I slip behind the wheel of my car, and Ostrander walks back into the grease jungle of his shop, ready to embark on yet another of his endless tasks.

When I call the Ostrander farm to set up an appointment with Anna May, the household is in crisis: Danny has been severely burned. He is in the hospital in critical condition, in a coma, hovering close to death. It is Saturday, and Ostrander, away for the weekend, has been contacted and is on his way home.

During the next week I call Ostrander's house on a regular basis. He is never in, but each day there is a new message on the machine with an update of Danny's condition. The messages are uniformly grim: still in a coma, in critical condition, on life support, doctors not sure if he'll make it, all we can do is hope and pray, thanks so much for all your support.

After about two weeks the message says that Danny has improved. He appears out of danger, though still on life support and the critical list, and responds to the nurse's voice. I leave a message asking Ostrander to call me back. He does at ten that night. We commiserate. I've kept clear of the rumors floating around town about how Danny managed to nearly get himself killed. I ask Ostrander to tell me the story.

He says Danny and Carl Peterson, a longtime friend, went to dinner at the Woodstock Pub. Danny, who has a reputation as a hard drinker with a wild streak, was steadily drinking. Peterson left him his car and rode home with a girlfriend.

Sometime later Danny fell asleep in Peterson's car. No

one knows how the fire started. The key was found in the "on" position. When the fire department arrived the car was smoking heavily. At first they didn't realize there was someone inside. Ostrander said if Danny had been pulled from the car even minutes later he would be dead. He was quickly admitted to New York Hospital's Cornell Burn Unit, one of the best of its kind in the world.

"He's tough as nails. In excellent physical condition. He's got that going for him," Ostrander says over the phone. He always knew in the back of his mind that something like this might happen. "He's got a lot of grit. Sometimes, I think, too much." In his voice is a mixture of love, concern, pride, resignation, and anger.

We discuss a date and time for a final interview with Anna May, whom he calls "Mother."

She calls him Alfred.

We are seated in one of the farmhouse's two downstairs living rooms chatting on a Wednesday afternoon. A Seth Thomas mantel clock, shaped like the boa constrictor that swallowed the elephant, ticks loudly on the mantel.

"He always said 'that clock needs winding. It's striking slow,' " Anna May says of her father-in-law, who the clock originally belonged to. "And I miss it. I miss it. I miss it when it's not striking."

Anna May is a small woman, sore afflicted with the Ostrander stoop. Large glasses dominate her face. These days she rarely leaves the house. "My eyes are not so good. I stumble around, and it angers me." Outings consist of Sunday church and an occasional foray for a pancake breakfast at the Lake Hill Firehouse.

While we chat Ostrander pops out to check on a minor "calamity." One of two 300-gallon gas tanks sprang a leak while he was conveying it from the Brockway. Petrol spurted over the truck's bed and dribbled out its gate. Wielding a hose and a fifty-gallon drum, he'd managed to contain the spill.

Anna May still wears a wedding band. I ask how she met Harry. She giggles with delight. "It was supper in the Shady Hall. I was sixteen when I met and seventeen when I married. At first I didn't know him from Adam." He gave her stationery and an envelope and told her to "write him a letter." He was twenty-five at the time. As Anna May tells it, his family pushed the match and she remained aloof for the longest time. Actually, as I find out later, the couple met in summer and were married in October 1928. Their courtship consisted of square dancing at the Franklin Store and Dance Hall in Lake Hill on Saturday nights. The marriage lasted fifty-seven years.

Ostrander reappears. "Seems like a fact of life. We're always smelling of grease or animal." He laughs, apologizing for the gasoline odor sneaking around the living room. A fair percentage of the five gallons which he expects to lose has soaked his clothing and boots. He lights a Marlboro. "Guess it can't be too bad. Lighting the cigarette I didn't blow myself up."

He is poised on the edge of the couch, not wanting to soil the upholstery with his work clothes; his posture also bespeaks a protectiveness toward Anna May. I ask how he is going to manage with Danny out of commission. He says he'll continue with the excavating and load the stockpile of logs Danny has pulled from the woods. Anna May remarks that logging is what Danny really liked to do, that he never cared much for "the excavating."

"He called it wearing out dirt," Ostrander says.

"Wearing out dirt?" I ask.

"Push it here. Push it there. Carry it. Put it down. Wear out dirt," he reiterates, smiling.

Anna May vigorously nods.

We move on to discuss Harry's character. "I'll tell you

he was a busy man," she says. "He was a self-made man. He'd tackle anything. There was no end to it." (I've long lost track of Harry's multiple enterprises.)

"By gosh! he was a cattle dealer. That was his life!" she exclaims, patting her hands against her lap. And later, talking of their Florida winter home, says "Harry hated it. Really and truly hated it. He couldn't wait to get back here. Everything was business. That was his life. To buy and sell."

I ask if it is okay for me to look around. After a moment's thought, Anna May says sure, cautioning me that her bed isn't made. In the other living room is a coyote Danny shot on Olderbark five years before, a VCR, and a gun laying across a chair. The coyote is stuffed and mounted on a pedestal with head tossed and fangs bared. The centerpiece of the spacious kitchen is a large, plastic-covered table which could easily sit eight.

The cordless phone rings. Ostrander hands it to Anna May, who talks for several minutes then explains that her sister-in-law just died of breast cancer and will be cremated over the weekend. The service is to be held in Black River near Watertown, five hours away. "I don't think I'll go," she says. The trip would be a major ordeal. "There's no viewing or anything. I feel sorry for my brother. But that's the way it is. It's a blessing she's gone."

I say goodbye to Anna May and walk through the waist-high timothy, wild grass, and white-and-purple clover to take some photos. From a hummock in the high pastures, the farm's views are shown to full advantage.

I meet Ostrander coming out of the barn. As we say goodbye I take a closer look at his big brass belt buckle—an inevitable fixture. He's had it for thirty years; a present from Jimmy John, who bought it at Shanty Store, an Army-Navy outlet on North Front and Fair Streets in Kingston, now defunct. The rectangular buckle is cast with an image of a long logging truck, stacked to the gills.

Once four stars surrounded red jewels in each corner, but the jewels are gone and only two faint stars remain. The truck is beginning to dissolve, like the old pennies my uncle used to give me—the coin smooth against my thumb, Lincoln's face a blur, the date barely decipherable.

6/22/90: "Good morning. This is Al Ostrander. It's Friday morning. If you're calling in regards to Danny's condition, he's still hanging in there, holding his own. He's heavily sedated so he doesn't thrash around and mess up his skin grafts. To use their term, he's out of it! When he's awake he's quite active, agitated, thrashing around. They're keeping him down. The lung situation is improving slightly [a pause]. That's it. If you want to leave your name and number, I'll try to get back to you. Thank you."

A RAMBLE INTO
THE WESTERN REACHES

I SPEED ALONG Route 28 over the crest of Pine Hill into
Delaware County. It's mid-July, the zenith of the summer.
Rain falls on and off. On National Public Radio, Ben
Bagdikian, professor of journalism at Berkeley, lectures
the Commonwealth Club of San Francisco on the perils
of media monopolies and easy credit. He says that he was
taught in the second grade that a penny saved is a penny
earned, and that we are all captives of our childhood.

Captives of our childhood. A neat phrase, I think, and
apt for my expedition. I'm going to Downsville, a place
I haven't been for over twenty years. As a child I was toted
this way by my parents—off to visit a mad English psychiatrist who lived in a big house and drove a vintage Rolls.
I am drawn along the same route we traveled, south and
west toward the Pennsylvania state line. Past Margaretville,
I turn onto Route 30. Through a thicket of trees I glimpse
the Pepacton Reservoir, a winding snake of water twenty
miles long and in most spots only a couple hundred yards
wide.

As a boy, I had heard that the Pepacton was fathom-
lessly deep and spawned trout big as torpedos; trout even
bigger than the ones that roamed the Ashokan; trout of
such magnitude that they could easily drag you off your
perch down into the reservoir's bottomless depths.

Such trout I never caught, though I fished the Pepacton
more than once. Line trailing into the gray water off the
steep embankment, I felt wary, feverish, and bored. I
invariably slept on the way home, drenched from the rain
that inevitably fell and bewildered by the twisted, in-
voluted valleys and the close hills rising without definition
or name.

Two decades later, the road unwinding in precisely the
same manner—water to the left, hunched hills right—I
scan my memory, waiting for the synapses to snap, the
associations to rise and break free, like a vibrant splash
against the white sky.

Recalcitrant, the past stays dim. Wildflowers bloom—
goldenrod, Queen Anne's lace, and white-and-purple
clover. A wakeful breeze bustles from the west. The sky
brightens and the dense trees dance. I pull over, stretch my
legs, and think of my father driving this stretch with a
station wagon full of kids. "Is pogo-sticking a fun sport?"
we chimed in unison, mimicking Bullwinkle the Moose.
The road to Downsville was enough to try any man's
patience without the impish choir. Once, he stopped
the car and threatened to leave us by the wayside. The
prospect of being stranded in the western wastes was
enough to shut any kid up. Even on this bright afternoon
there is a spookiness about the empty road, the drowned
valley, and the low, thick trees.

Almost a century ago, John Burroughs recorded his
impressions of this valley in a travelogue titled "A Summer Voyage." Burroughs feels the mid-summer pull of the
Delaware's southward flow. He builds a boat and floats
downstream, living off milk from local farmers, berries,

and trout. He describes his feelings as night comes on:

> In the woods, things are close to you, and you touch
> them and seem to interchange something with them;
> but upon the river...you are more isolated, farther
> removed from the soil and its attractions, and an easier
> prey to unsocial demons. The long, un-peopled vistas
> ahead; the still, dark eddies; the endless monotone and
> soliloquy of the stream; the unheeding rocks basking
> like monsters along the shore...a solitary heron starting
> up here and there, as you round some point, and flap-
> ping disconsolately ahead till lost to view, or standing
> like a gaunt specter on the umbrageous side of the
> mountain...

An image of a skeletal bird in shadow. Burroughs felt the
haunting of this valley, as I do now.

Even someone as prosaic as Richard Smith, surveyor
and land speculator, who traveled here two centuries ago
has nothing good to say about the place. Smith recorded
his impressions of the Upper Delaware in a journal recently reissued by Purple Mountain Press with the title *A Tour
of the Hudson, the Mohonk, the Susquehanna, and the
Delaware in 1769*. He writes that most of the upper
Delaware is "all stoney, broken, barren and of little worth.
The Timber down to the Popaghton is mostly Beech,
Maple, Hemloc, Butternut & Buttonwood.... We agree that
the Delaware can-not compare with the Susquehanna for
good Land; nor is the Timber much more than Half as
tall."

Smith was looking to invest, to sail timber down river,
cultivate cash crops, and buy himself an Assembly seat.
He's part and parcel of the grand colonial rigmarole—
the original gentrification. Because Smith spent much of
his time recording the landscape's resources, his ethno-
graphic observations are summary; he does, however,

manage to convey the squalid misery of aboriginal life: the smoking fires, filthy huts, and ragged clothing that no amount of retrospective romanticizing could ever change. A typical colonialist, Smith calls the Indians lazy, indolent, and idle. Nevertheless, he acknowledges that "they are faithful in all they undertake, have sharp Eyesight, surprising Knowledge of the Woods, are expert in hunting, fishing, managing Canoes, and in whatever else they have been conversant."

While Smith remarks that the Delaware lacked personal property (as though that were the defining characteristic branding them primitive), he acknowledges that they had very definite ideas of territory. Their eighteenth-century boundaries had been defined by a history of conquest and subjugation (the tribal may have a higher degree of internal communality but is finally just as insular, possessive, and xenophobic as any of today's societies). Smith, explaining the Indians's presence on the continent, mentions a migration across the Bering Straits, a theory that I have always thought the provenance of twentieth-century anthropology.

As I drive into Downsville two centuries after Smith's survey, my mind is on my father at the helm of his little clan. He never stopped in Downsville, but pushed on. Where was he going? And why?

The psychiatrist practiced behind two padded doors, where his patients slept with a tape recorder under their pillows subliminally planting messages in their brains. The house was always full of strange people—demented heirs and blocked geniuses. He injected his patients with hallucinogenic cocktails. In my mind he will always appear as an eviscerated syringe with a shock of grizzled hair. One snowy night he skidded his Rolls off the road into someone's living room. I envision his eyes frozen behind steelrimmed spectacles and the car gliding as though with a mind of its own into the snowy night. The Rolls was called, I think, a Silver Ghost.

As I flit about Downsville, (manicured, quiet, and genteelly well-maintained), I feel the pull of the Pennsylvania boonies, a true back country where such weirdness could flourish unchecked. I stop briefly to refuel. "Where's the road to Roscoe?" I ask the attendant. "Two miles back. Up Cat Hollow."

I realize I'm still inclined to feel like an interloper in Downsville. An image appears of street lamps ringed by haloes as seen through the cold car windows blotted with my finger marks. The heater whirs and I'm close to sleep. I hesitate another moment, admiring the wide lawns under the old trees in full leaf, before hightailing it east to fish the famous Beaverkill.

Cat Hollow turned out to be a picturesque little pass running between low mountains with names like Campbell, Brock, and Morton Hill. After twenty minutes I pulled into Roscoe; it was mid-afternoon. I joked with four kids waiting for their mother to emerge from the supermarket then drove out of town and asked directions to the no-kill section of the river. As I began fishing, I could see why the Beaverkill is fabled. In many sections its bottom is covered with wide, horizontal stones that are compacted and full of fissures and ledges.

My wiles that afternoon were insufficient to make the sly fish rise; perhaps they had been hauled in and fondled one too many times. I didn't persevere. The public access to the Beaverkill—home of fly-fishing in America—is now paralleled by an equally public four-lane highway bearing traffic from the Hudson Valley through the Delaware into the Susquehanna and then onward to the small mid-state cities of Binghamton and Elmira; the upper part of the Beaverkill, before it joins the Willomec, is owned by private clubs.

I took a roundabout way back to Downsville, making

a cursory loop through East Branch, a pleasantly desolate place, so named because the east branch of the Delaware joins the Beaverkill just outside town. East Branch is blessed with lumber and stone yards and wide streets. I saw no stores, restaurants, or bars and thought that perhaps I was in the wrong place, a satellite of East Branch actual, an isolate offshoot of the town itself. I didn't stick around to find out but took off north and east on Route 30, which parallels the Delaware, where long, calm flats sided by rushes meant hard fishing, definitely out of my league.

I pulled up in front of the Shinhopple country store. "Hello my friend!" said the man behind the counter as I entered. He was in his sixties, white-haired, and beaming.

"So, what's new in Shinhopple?" I asked as I moved toward the glass cooler in the rear.

"What's new! What's new! Lots new here!" he said.

Back at the register, we had a little chat about night fishing on the east branch, old farms in the area bought up and portioned off, and the Brownsville section of Brooklyn where he spent his youth.

"Goy or yid?" he said to me, eyes shifting down and inward. I was reminded that I was on the edge of the Borscht Belt. Around the same period we went to the psychiatrist's home we also went to the ritzy Jewish resorts of Brown's, Grossinger's, Kutcher's, and the Concord. For every grand hotel there were scores of boarding houses, cabins, bungalows, and hideaways.

"A quarter, a quarter, and a deuce," he said, counting out my change, a rummy player to the last.

Back in Downsville, I inspected a covered bridge, then drove back to the Esopus Creek, where I fished on and off till dusk, mostly off. I was fascinated by an old man in hip waders casting with grace and alacrity. His delight as he landed the trout that he regularly caught was a pleasure to behold. A young man (whom I took to be his grandson) stood before him, slightly intimidated but nonetheless eager for a cast. But the old man wouldn't let up, and I didn't blame him.

A week later I was back on the western tier. I'd driven north along the Schoharie Valley, through Hunter, Lexington, and Prattsville, where I stopped to eat in a homey roadside diner exuding vintage Eisenhower narcolepsy. The pie was good. After lunch I crossed Main Street, drifted through a lot stacked with railroad ties, foraged in a patch of ripe raspberries, and waded a small tributary. The Schoharie River glinted through the trees: a hundred feet wide and shallow, the water sliding downhill in tangents and oblique angles. I settled on the rocky shore and, while flies sucked my blood, surveyed the shifting water and let my mind go blank.

Back in town, I stopped at a local real estate office. Paul Brody, who grew up in Woodstock (and after several disastrous romances fled to Greene County), gave me the lowdown on real estate in Prattsville, Conesville, and Grand Gorge. A builder, Brody said none of the locals in the area could afford anything but modular homes and trailers. Land in western Greene County sells for $7,000 an acre, Brody said, adding that that's cheap by Windham standards. He said most home buyers were city weekenders in their fifties and sixties, a retirement crowd.

I mulled this over as I headed west out of town. I wondered why I found the idea of the second home so abhorrent. Aristotle said the city is the locus of civilization—it separates a society from savagery. But today I think that for cities generally, and New York particularly, that maxim has reversed. City people nowadays are the prototypes of a new barbarian—wallowing in a foul sty, blithely side-stepping living corpses, slaves to mercenary economics.

It's an old story, city mouse/country mouse, and I tried to see it in that light. But philosophy aside, it irked me to no end that city pressure was coming to bear on the rolling farmland between Grand Gorge and Stamford. It was driving land prices up, disassembling the country.

The landscape still sustained silos, patchwork fields of corn and new-mown hay, cattle ranging over the hillsides, and white clapboard farmhouses set beside dirt roads. I stopped briefly in Stamford (where a deranged young man had recently killed his family) and snapped some pictures. At the first traffic light I headed south on Route 10. The country was all farmland, lush fields, and the smell of manure. To the east, the boundary of the rugged interior range of the Catskills—Utsayantha, McGregor, Plattekill, and Pisgah Mountains, with elevations of over 3,000 feet—gave way to gentler hills.

I stopped at the public access to the headwaters of the west branch of the Delaware River, put together my fly rod, climbed over a little step that the Department of Environmental Conservation had apparently put there for the angler's convenience, and followed a prim footpath toward the river, several hundred yards distant.

Soon I was thrashing through the edge of a cornfield snarled with brush over my head. The devilishly uneven terrain was full of potholes, sinks, and invisible chasms into which I constantly lurched and fell. Pollen from the numerous flowers shaken by my passage swirled into my face, racking me with sneezes and half blinding my tearing eyes.

I nearly fell face first into a swampy morass that soaked me past the shins. My hair was a tangle of twigs and crawling insects. Consoling myself with the thought that I was about to fish water that few had mucked, I pushed on. Brambles ripped at my neck and arms. When I finally made the stream I realized, much to my disgust, that on the other side of the small creek was a patch through open fields which I simply hadn't seen. At least I knew the return trip would be a breeze. And before me a tempting pool swirled under an old willow. I fished the west branch, wading through riffles, casting my fly into eddies and undercut banks, raising a dozen small fish but hooking none. The current pulled at my ankles, reminding me of Loren Eisley's beautiful essay about floating down the Platte, borne on the gentle tilt of the continent.

The west branch slipped downhill. I looked south, imagining the Delaware water gap, the jagged sickle of the river carved into the edge of the eastern seaboard. I thought of the river's lower reaches, where it sprawls, polluted and fouled by more than runoff from farms. The water tugged; I felt its pull, cool below my knees.

I walked back through a freshly mown field, where high pastures wrapped over the ridgelines. The ground was rife with clover, and honeybees drifted on the wind. A yellow finch darted from the hedges. Two ebony butterflies with iridescent green wings airily hopped in tandem. I drove through Delhi, picked up Route 28 near its source and followed it eastward back to Mount Tremper, Willow Lakehill, and home.

A couple of weeks after my excursion to the west branch, I rambled once more into the western reaches. I thought: Enough of this mad driving and fishing; nothing is more stultifying than a motor tour. I determined that this would be my last exploration into Delaware County. I wanted to concentrate on one place, and chose Bovina.

Why Bovina, you might ask. Well, since Delaware County is dairy-farm country, Bovina seemed an appropriate finale. It's also off the beaten track, tucked away between Andes and Delhi. I hoped to find a quiet little hamlet with its own character and charm, and I was not disappointed.

I took the long drive out along Route 28 one Thursday morning in early August. I cruised along at a leisurely pace, determined not to push it, not to rush. I wanted to relax and attain a convivial, unhurried frame of mind with which to encounter my sleepy little backwater.

My first stop was Russell's, the only store in town, where the rather elderly and breathless proprietress, Marjorie Wilson, showed off her penny-candy case. "Can't buy that in the city," she boasted. The store itself was an imbroglio of groceries, dry goods, clothing, old bills piled on antique desks, writing pads, cosmetics, and bathroom supplies all strung out in two rows under whirling fans. The place had an air of both clutter and want.

I walked over to the post office behind the United Presbyterian Church. The sermon for the week was "Stress: Out of Control?" The cicadas buzzed, and I found myself yawning. Postmaster Pat Parsons told me that Bovina is the smallest township in Delaware County with some 560 souls, according to the 1980 census.

I drove out into the countryside, passing farms, pastureland, and ponds and headed up into the hills. I stopped at the end of a long dead-end road on the side of Mount Pisgah and watched a badger, ten pounds of pure muscle with a stance like a fullback, lumber off into the brush. The views were of farm after farm rolling west.

Back in town I dropped in on Hugh Lee, an artist that Diane Galusha, editor of the *Catskill Mountain News*, had mentioned as one of Bovina's prominent citizens. Lee—slight, white-haired, and pale, with a dry, unfaltering gaze—lived in a house built in the early nineteenth-century set on a hill in the middle of town. He said he was Bovina's justice of the peace, as well as, "reluctantly," its town historian.

In his capacity as historian, Lee said that he spent much of his time tracing family trees for the Daughters of the American Revolution. I viewed a few of his paintings scattered about the house. "I love Bovina," he said, and told me that eighteen years earlier he had become fed up with New York and took a job as director of graphics at the State University in Delhi for half the money he was making in advertising. He's never looked back.

Lee told me that Jack Burns—the largest dairier left in town, whose family has been farming in the area since the 1820s—was milking his cows down the road. I headed off to see the industry that had given Bovina its name.

Burns looked the part of scion from the prime Scottish stock that had originally settled the area. "Scottish thrift and Scottish piety have transmitted traits that do honor to the children of the countrymen of Scott and Wallace," says a late-nineteenth-century account of the town. Burns had a Scot's flared bushy eyebrows, ruddy complexion, and hardworking air.

I met him in the "well" of his milking room. Half a dozen cows were penned against each wall, the black octopi of the automatic milking machines sucking at their udders. The well, floored with yellow plastic matting, was set below where the cows stood—massive Holsteins, 1,400–1,500 pounds each, Burns told me. He moved up and down the well, hooking the cows to the machine that pumped their milk into a large holding tank in an adjoining room, working the three hanging coils that spurted a blue bacteria-killing solution onto each animal's udder after she'd voided.

Burns owns over 100 cows and about 700 acres. He usually doesn't do the milking himself, but that day his milker was out sick. I met several other hired hands: shy men who rise at four each morning and finish their day at six at night. Burns said he ships 14,000 pounds of milk every other day. I waded through the manure, inspected the barn, and let a new-born calf suck on my fingers.

Burns and I had a glass of milk from the holding tank. The milk was white and cold and thick. Not pasteurized, not homogenized, and absolutely delicious. That glass brought back the summer sixteen years before when I worked on a dairy farm across the Hudson. "Not bad," said Burns, cocking an eyebrow.

I drove back that evening through New Kingston. As I peaked the crest of the Esopus watershed just east of Belleayre, I thought about the night my family had driven back from Pennsylvania after visiting that mad shrink. It had just finished snowing, and a few flakes still swirled in the air. We started down the snowy grade above Pine Hill in the big station wagon. Suddenly, the car was spinning clockwise, round and round, in slow motion, drifting gently downhill, smack in the middle of the road. To this day, I remember my father braking when the car was at a diagonal. My friend, slightly older than I was, counted the spins; I recall three-and-a-half full revolutions in all. It was late at night, and no one else was on the road. We came to a full stop crosswise in the middle of the road and thanked our lucky stars.

This experience remains clear—the wonder of it, its surreal attenuation, the lack of fear. That clockwise whirling was the image I had been searching for when I began my rambles to the western reaches. It was the embodiment of time, time which moves in only one direction. Movement into the past (the ramifying glass of milk, the madeleine) is literary, fictive.

I sped down the long straight hill, going home.

THE WIDOWS OF DINGLE HILL

AN OLD MAN WITH A drooping mustache and cloudy eyes
first told me about Dingle Hill. "You want to see the country like it was? That's the place to go," he said.

Soon after, I was speaking to a woman with great feeling for the Catskills. She said the backwater south of Andes
was untouched—old farms off narrow dirt roads with
grass growing up the middle. Homesteads unchanged for
a hundred years. "I've seen many beautiful places in these
mountains, but this is something special."

I had sworn off rambling the Catskills's western
reaches after a series of stupefying and unsuccessful
fishing tours during July and August through Downsville,
Stamford, Delhi, and Bovina. Never again, I vowed.

But imagining quaint couples rocking on porches
welcoming me home like a prodigal child, I felt myself
wavering. Fresh-baked berry pie would be set out to
cool on a wide kitchen table; I could taste coffee and
cream. And, over a reluctant third piece of pie, the past
of these mountains that I've chosen to call home would

be unveiled. The farmer would recount walking to a dance in Hamden Town, coming home as the harvest moon set and dew coated the meadow grass like resin. I could see him kicking along, a young man, neck open to the weather. His mother would have baked a blackberry pie for his return. He'd stand in the big kitchen in the pale pre-dawn and wolf it down.

I found the scenario compelling. Delving through my maps, I saw that the area between the north shore of the Pepacton Reservoir and Andes looked bereft of settlements or major thoroughfares—in fact, anything that would distinguish it in the eyes of the world. I was hooked and so it was that I found myself once again following Route 28 into Delaware County.

Dingle, dingle, I mused as I drove along. According to my dictionary, a dingle is a "small wooded valley; dell." I ran Dylan Thomas's lines like honey over my tongue:

> The night above the dingle starry,
> Time let me hail and climb
> Golden in the heyday of his eyes

Thomas wrote about Wales, not the western Catskills; but one dingle is as good as another, I reasoned. For Thomas, the word connoted country sleep, a charmed warbling, the intimacy of rolling hills. As I whizzed through the New World, dingle had a different feel. Ding. Dingy. Dingbat. Dingo. Dingus! The root seemed infused with inconsequence, slightly aggravating but nonetheless endearing. A word with good Middle English origin; none of that stuffy Latin, tongue-twisting Greek, pretentious French, bastardized German, or mournful Norse. Dingle: an honest word for honest folk.

Ding, ding, ding. A southerly wind buffeted the trees, and the small car swayed. I wound through the vales west of Margaretville where 28 narrows, twisting and turning

up the crooked cleft of Palmer Hollow. The hardwoods
swept upward studded with hemlock, the dell a twilight
green. Behind me a new compact car filled the rearview
mirror. City folks, I thought, rushing to make the most
of their precious country weekend, which they had paid
for up the wazoo. Hurrying to relax. I pulled over and
let them pass.

Dipping down the long hill to Andes, I wondered what
impelled those who named Andes, Delhi, and Tunis Lake.
As I cruised into town, I thought perhaps they drew them
out of a hat holding other possibilities like Madagascar,
Rangoon, Hiroshima, and Saigon.

I stopped opposite Vincent's County Cafe and sat for
a long moment, staring like a zombie out the opaque
windshield. The car's engine made little clicks and pings.
Rain swished down. I collected my rambling parapher-
nalia: a 5 x 8–inch, ruled yellow pad; my 35-millimeter,
point-and-shoot camera given to me two years before on
my birthday in Japan by a wealthy Buddhist priest who'd
taken a liking to my wife when they met swimming in a
north Tokyo spa; a number of pens, all of which I disliked
in varying degrees; and maps of Delaware County that
I'd characteristically managed to mangle. I walked across
to the cafe for lunch.

Inside I was greeted by a convivial hum. Under the
hanging globes of 1950s lamps, seated on barstools around
the red Formica counter, it seemed that everyone knew
everyone. Delaware dairymen steeped in the odors of
livestock and manure lumbered toward the bathroom to
wash their hands. They mingled with small town realtors
and bankers in cheap jackets, wash-and-wear shirts, and
polyester ties. Three generations of women all looking
turned out by the same beauty parlor munched with blank
faces on burgers and chips.

I ate my sandwich and eavesdropped on the small-
town gossip. A hard-faced waitress in her mid-forties with

dyed blond hair, mascara, and soft white arms handled the floor solo, taking flack from a plump male cook with curly graying hair and an earring. I thought the earring was incongruous for a town like Andes. A woman I took to be the cook's wife entered, trailing two kids. She'd managed to retain a sultry air. The atmosphere was suddenly full of illicit tinglings. On the radio, Don Henley sang:

> Offer up your best defense
> This is the end
> of the innocence.

I was getting too wrapped up in the scene's subtext. A plastic case was stocked with deep-dish blueberry, peach, and apple pies. I was already full. And, besides, pie awaited me—the proverbial pie set out for the stranger, the wayfarer, the unbidden guest, the prodigal child returned.

The register dinged, and the cash drawer banged shut. I left a large tip as futile compensation for my voyeurism and stepped out onto Andes's uneven pavements. The rain had eased, but the sky still whisked low over the church spires, refabricating itself moment by moment.

Where 28 turns toward Delhi I went straight on, heading west along County Route 2 toward the border of Hamden Town. Stone walls rose with the road that did not devolve into a forgotten country lane as I had expected. The speed limit was 55 mph. This is no good, I thought. Not at all what I had in mind. A small byway branched to the right. "Dead end," said the sign. The road pitched down. I passed a trailer, a modular home, and a driveway leading to a vintage 1970s local builder's second home. An instant countryman special: vertical composition siding; long, thin windows; cramped quarters; the smell of rot—not exactly old farmsteads.

A hundred yards in, a young couple in a small yellow car with a broken windshield pulled over to let me pass.

Further along I found a barn, shored up but still decomposing. Blackberry bushes sprawled into the road. A big maple hugged a stone wall; perhaps a hundred years ago a farmer had fancied it and spared it from the ax. Heavy goldenrod stamen drooped everywhere, pregnant with pollen. Two snow-white geese toddled into the sumac and scrub.

The road had turned level and bad. I noticed a dozen junked cars, hoods sprung, half hidden by grass. I came to a trailer and waited in the car. No one emerged. Turned around, I spotted the yellow car coming toward me around the barn. It pulled over, ducking behind brush, out of sight. Apprehensive, I drove slowly out of the cul-de-sac. The place reeked of parsimony. Better days. The yellow car lay in wait.

As I slipped past, the driver cracked his window and called, so I stopped. He got out of the car and walked over.

"Looking for someone?" he said. He was in his late twenties, and had sleep-tousled hair and narrow eyes.

I felt on edge and gave him the name of an L.A. friend.

"Don't know anyone down here like that," he said shaking his head. "Just me and my brother. Most people come down here looking for me or my brother. You looking for us?"

I told him I wasn't.

" 'Course most folks coming down here in nice cars like this," he said, "are lost."

"What happened to your windshield?"

"Softball smashed it in Delhi," he said, spat, and shuffled. He looked over the sagging outbuildings. "Me and my brother are the only two left. Most people coming down here are looking for me and my brother."

I was tempted to pursue the conversation. This young man and his brother probably had something to tell, and most likely something to sell. I still felt uneasy, however, and decided to pass. Goodbyes were exchanged, and I drove on, away from the broken-down farm and leaving the two brothers to cope with the neglected land.

I turned off Route 2, this time onto Wolf Hollow Road, which looked recently resurfaced. I soon found out why. Much of the surrounding acreage had been parcelled off and sold. Small driveways branched like exploratory borings from a main shaft. Wolf Hollow hit Turkey Hollow, which joined Skunk Hollow and Fish Hollow. I stuck to the Wolf, bearing south, gently dropping toward the Pepacton Reservoir. Gradually, as I went deeper into the hollow, development tapered off. The car moved along slowly in first gear, drawn by its own weight downward. I gazed contentedly at the profusion of wildflowers and ferns and drifted through a leafy arbor, taking my ease, going I knew not where.

It seemed Wolf Hollow went on forever. Ponds began to appear by the roadside, jet disks banded by grass. Dead tree trunks thrust into the flocculent sky like bony fingers. I stopped driving and turned off the engine. Steep hills flared on either side. The wind smelled of autumn. I knew it from long ago—full of apples, first frost, and light that raced away. Soon the air would be of little weight. I thought of Richard Hugo's lines:

> Listen, Paula. Feel. This wind has traveled
> all the way around the world, picked up heat
> from the Sahara, a new Tasmanian
> method of love, howl of the arctic whale.

Small raindrops nipped my cheeks. A profound silence reigned. I stood bewitched. Crows cawed. The wind sighed and fell. Then it began to rain in earnest. I tilted my face to the sky and closed my eyes.

I brought myself back from the cool patter of countless feet and dimming calls of the carrion eaters. I sat for a moment before turning the car key, following the rain's rhythmic click against the roof, savouring its coolness on my eyelids and lips. Then I drove on. The Hollow cupped a small stream. Soon a one-lane bridge spanned the Tremper Kill, and the country lay down in fields of rolling corn.

Turning north on County Route 1, I headed for Dingle Hill proper. A rickety farm stand, manned by grasshoppers, offered only several dozen ears of old corn. It marked the head of Dingle Hill Road. A historical marker indicated that it was one mile to the scene of the "tragedy" of under-sheriff Osman N. Steele, who was slain by anti-renters in August 1845.

In his definitive history, *The Catskills*, Alf Evers sees the slaying of Steele by the Calico Indians (white men in disguise) and the subsequent trial as the culmination of the anti-rent war (tenant farmers rebelling against absentee landlords with perpetual leases). Steele, by Evers's account, was pompous and abusive; his death was the catalyst that both sobered the anti-rent movement and led to land law reforms.

One man's death was all it took to tip the scales. Perhaps Steele was a hero in spite of himself; or was his death pointless? On the job the night he was killed, Steele was supervising the sale of a Calico's cattle for back rent. His wife was at his side when he died and was carried to a nearby farmhouse one hot summer night over a century ago on Dingle Hill.

That day no visible agitation stirred. Farming machinery stood out by a barn and an old, white farmhouse with potted flowers set out on its broad stone steps. Evergreens shaded the stoop. A white-haired woman answered the door. Reluctantly, she bade me enter. We talked in the dim light of the front parlor.

She said she bought this farm with her husband when they moved to Dingle Hill from Roxbury in 1942. She had grown up farming. Her husband had died a while back and now her son dairied on their 350 acres. "We have ninety head all together, what with the heifers and all."

As we talked further it was evident that this farm girl, an eighty-two-year-old widow, had prospered in real estate. After selling the old farm in Roxbury, she bought it back when the bank foreclosed and then resold to the people who developed Roxbury Run. A number of other deals were mentioned.

"It's all cut up," she said when I asked if there were any original homesteads on Dingle Hill. I asked how she felt about the dissolution of the kind of life she'd grown up with. She glared at me, shrewd and annoyed; the conversation was at an end. I asked her name; she gave it, but as she ushered me out the door said "No way, shape, or matter will you use my name. I refuse. If I see it in print, I'll..." She let it hang.

Before leaving, I managed to pry directions to a another widow who she said was the only native left on Dingle Hill that hadn't picked up, sold out, or died. "Go up over the hill and then down. Bear right, drive for a ways, bear right. When you come to a bridge bear right again. Her place in on the hill. Should take you twenty to twenty-five minutes. Her name is Min Carelli."

It was uncanny. I never doubted I would find Min Carelli. I turned out the driveway and headed uphill with the utmost confidence. Dales half hidden by mist, I rose over the farm. The sky was an ashen caul with a brightness behind it that hurt my eyes. I began to brood as I drove along on what was becoming an obsessive theme since I had returned to the Catskills. As I crested Dingle Hill, I saw the sort of house that the car I had let pass in Palmer Hollow was speeding toward—not the glass and cedar palaces of Woodstock, but rather a smaller place, more in keeping with the three-plus hours it took to drive from the city. The extra distance has kept prices down. (The widow had told me that she was selling a thirty-acre woodlot on this hilltop for $30,000, which is unheard of in my neck of the woods.)

It wasn't the inflated prices around Woodstock that irked me, or the accompanying hype. What rankled me was a fundamental dislike of New York City and a basic distrust of almost anyone who would choose to live there.

The archeologist, anthropologist, historiographer, and great Mayan scholar Robert Redfield discusses this basic aversion in a book titled *The Primitive World and Its Transformations*. One of the "principle frontiers of every civilization" is the division between city and country, he says. In his essay "Civilization and the Moral Order," Redfield struggles to understand the reason for this demarcation, which is almost as though our social being had been halved, split like a peach to reveal some hard fissured pit of adversity within:

> It is not possible rightly to suppose that the precivilized age was distinguished by the important presence of the missionary or prophet. The preacher of conversion and the preacher of moral regeneration are creatures of civilization. It is through the city that the many moral orders confined to small local communities become something to be defended, struggled for, remade.

An interesting notion. A codification of the dogma I espoused. I was caught up in a secularized but nonetheless claustrophobic rant against degeneracy. As I saw it, there should be an implicit *quid pro quo*. For the country necessities of life the city returned culture, the manufacture of imaginative possibilities. But where is that culture today? What possibilities does it offer?

I'd like to think that the future holds smaller and self-sufficient cities that are more in touch with landscape and their sources of nourishment. Cities that would generate their own power and recycle their waste. I realize this may be an unrealistic ideal: The world becomes increasingly crowded; cities enlarge. But I'm convinced that the last vestiges of civilization will be in what country remains— those who hold sacred the air they breathe, the water they drink, and the land.

On Dingle Hill, a subdued example of the embattled frontier, it was getting darker. I dropped into the dell in late afternoon, carapace of charcoal haze descending. A fortyish man with a petrified pompadour and garish tatoos on his forearms was busy about his yard.

"Know where I can find Min Carelli?" I asked. He cupped his hand to his ear, a scowl of contempt and impatience fixing his face. "Must be a newcomer," he said, when I repeated the name, and turned away.

"She's supposed to be a widow with an old farm who won't sell."

"Mincarelli!" He looked at me like I was crazy and pointed up the ridge. "Right there."

I crossed a small bridge and climbed the backside of the hill. The driveway to Mincarelli's place was framed with flowers. An old barn stood near a small spic-and-span white house. Out back was the garden where I met Mrs. Mincarelli, a small, stocky woman with a hoarse voice, harvesting tomatoes and zucchini. Her family had descended on her (she made it sound unexpected) for the Labor Day weekend.

"What you want know? I got nothing to say." She spoke with a thick Italian accent.

I introduced myself. The savory smells of garlicky tomato sauce wafted out of the kitchen door to where we stood talking.

When I told her who had given me her name, she pointed to her temple. "She's a smart lady. She make a lotta money in real estate. What she talking about? She been here longer than me. She come in '42. My husband

and me come in '48. So much work," she said, describing dairying when the milk truck still made the Dingle Hill run.

I asked Mincarelli why she hadn't sold out. "I'm not gonna sell ten acres here, fifteen acres there. By the time you go to the lawyer, what you got left? What else we got but land? I leave it to my family."

It started to pour, so I followed her into the house. Pictures of the Last Supper and the Crucifixion were on the walls. She showed off a wedding photo taken in the '30s. In a long white dress with flowers in her hair, Mincarelli was beautiful, her husband young and dashing. "So small. Just like a little girl," she said, pinching at her waist and tilting her head.

I took photos of her and her son Sonny, who lived in Pennsylvania and was fixing a weed eater.

On the way back to Andes, I stopped on the top of Dingle Hill and looked west over rolling fields and the farm below. On the radio, an evangelist was talking about the decay of the flesh and the ignorance of the unsaved. "When you're going down for the third time what do you say," he asked rhetorically. I got out of the car. The rain had eased. I took a couple of deep breaths, and Thomas's voice sang on the wind:

And then to awake, and the farm, like a wanderer white
With the dew, come back, the cock on his shoulder: it was all
Shining, it was Adam and maiden,
The sky gathered again
And the sun grew round that very day.
So it must have been after the birth of the simple light
In the first, spinning place

"The first spinning place" echoed in my mind as I drove away. I had the premonition that those lines would be with me when I died, from the first spinning place to the aperture's close. Would I too leave a woman behind? I passed through Andes without stopping at the cafe for the homemade pie that I had somehow missed.

Through Palmer Hollow, heading toward Margaretville, mist rose from the unbroken forest. I pulled to the roadside and took photos. Cars ticked past me carrying the Labor Day traffic west. Should I go back? I wondered. Should I try to find those untouched farms and the sleepy backwaters? Should I try to find the front porch of my adopted home? Crows cawed at arbitrary intervals. The uplands of the big mountains were shrouded in clouds.

CRUMP CASTLE

HAVING GROWN UP IN the Catskills, I think it's odd that I'd never been to Pine Hill. The town always seemed like a nonentity—a jumble of roofs buried under Route 28 where it climbs toward Bellayre. I was unprepared for the hamlet's charm as I drove down Main Street one sleepy day in August. I was on my way to Crump Castle. It's ruins, I'd heard, were one the Catskills's forgotten wonders.

Townsfolk wafted in and out of the post office. Trendy eateries mingled with quiescent rooming houses. I asked for directions to the local sporting-goods store from a man in his early forties. He was so amiable that I decided to explore the town itself before ranging in the hinterlands.

Feeling a bit conspicuous I locked up (did people lock their cars in Pine Hill?). I walked down Main Street and paused in front of the Colonial Inn. The building had deteriorated but retained a funky majesty. On the front porch, behind a row of saddles, an elderly woman stared at the world through dimming eyes. I wanted a photo. Seeking permission, I ducked inside.

Innkeeper Mrs. Witte directed me "out back" to speak to her husband. I found Steve Witte, a workhorse of a man, clambering over a mountain of cut wood, chain saw in hand. A shirtless youth stood atop the pile, arms folded across his chest. Behind us raw fields sloped upward to a fence row. I was again conscious of how Pine Hill set.

Witte pulled earplugs and killed the saw. Glad for the break, he began to chat. The inn had at one time served as a stage stop for the run from Kingston to Delhi. Witte's hanging sign said 1870, but part of the building was older, probably from the early 1800s.

When I asked about Crump Castle, the young man told me that he'd been there the night before "looking around to see where my sister was." He said "Nazi signs" were scrawled on the Castle's walls and that the place was haunted. Witte introduced him as his son, Steve, Jr. Witte pooh-poohed the swastikas, which he said might be Buddhist symbols. "The place is in dire need of repair," he added, gazing around at his own building and grounds. I accompanied him inside, and when we were out of earshot of Steve, Jr., Witte confided that his daughter had indeed snuck out the night before.

The Colonial's interior was loaded with an eclectic assortment of antiques, trophies, and furniture in varying styles (from hunting lodge to mafioso kitch). I inspected a vintage Bengal stove while questioning Witte on his background. He'd owned the Colonial for nine years, moved up from the boroughs and had come to the Catskills often as a child.

I don't know how we started talking about fishing, but in no time I found myself sitting on a plush blue wraparound sofa watching homemade videos of brown trout heading up the Delaware's east branch. Scanning forward for particularly telling shots, Witte explained that at this time of year the Pepacton trout either go deep or head upstream to escape the warming reservoir. The tape froze; thirty-inch brown trout hovered in the current.

Witte definitely had my interest at that point. The more I looked, the more agitated I became. I despaired of ever catching such fish. Witte talked slowly and with effort, like a man in chains splitting stones. The fish swirled and then held steady in two feet of water. They looked lethal—big enough to eat a kitten.

I confessed that I was resigned to being old and gray before cracking the Esopus's secrets. Witte sympathized. "Go out in the early morning. Evenings you don't really knock 'em dead." Predictable advice that nonetheless cheered me up. The comely daughter appeared, her manner both shy and curious.

Before I left, Witte produced a history of Pine Hill by Nancy T. Smith, Shandaken's town historian. He offered to lend it to me, but I said that I'd buy a copy. He directed me to the gun shop of Smith's husband, Charlie.

Charlie Smith's shop was housed in a long white trailer. On its side a sign proclaimed: "SHARPENED— circle saws, scissors, saw chain, mower blades, handsaws, carbide saws, knives, clipper blades and much more." Inside were guns of all makes and vintages. A stuffed bobcat crouched on a back counter. Smith—middle-aged, bearded, wide shouldered—is Pine Hill's justice of the peace as well as a gun dealer. He shook my hand and gladly sold me a copy of his wife's book, but said he didn't know much about Crump. Seemed no one did.

Two young women, tough-looking and provocative, entered the shop. One wore a black camisole, cut midriff, that was tight across her breasts and exposed a flat stomach. Her hair was dark and cut boot camp–style, except for a whip snaking down into the hollow of her back. She did all the talking. Her companion—tall, blond, full-bodied—stood with her hands on her hips, chin held high, thrusting out her chest. I was tempted to stay, but their business seemed private.

"I was wondering if you could give us a little advice, Charlie. My friend has a problem," said the dark one as I was going out the door.

I found Mrs. Smith as promised at the Shandaken Historical Museum putting the final touches on a quilt exhibition. She impressed me as an eminently respectable woman who would have made an exemplary teacher in the defunct elementary school which housed the museum.

What a couple the Smiths made! He, the burly, gun-shop judge with a twinkle in his eye. She—from an old Shandaken family—a crusader working to preserve the region's heritage. It was hard to tell where she left off and her mission began. They both seemed so involved and plugged in. So fully a part of small-town society.

While I perused the museum's permanent exhibition, Nancy rummaged through her files for Crump photos. One particular display caught my eye: Crystal Spring, a turn-of-the-century Pine Hill bottled-water operation. The promotional brochure boasted that the spring turned out 4,500 gallons a minute at a constant forty-two degrees, summer and winter. Sixty-five cents bought a case of six big bottles, or a five-gallon demijohn. A fire in 1919 destroyed the business. I wondered if it could be revived as a cottage industry.

Mrs. Smith said the spring still supplied Pine Hill's water. I sat in her cluttered office as she riffled her files for Crump photos. Eventually she found a thin envelope of 2″ x 2″ black-and-white shots of sculptures and wrought iron. She said most of the castle's art and architectural detail had since been pillaged. I asked her about the legends Crump spawned. About these she knew nothing. She gave me Forest Dutcher's name, a former president of the Shandaken Gun Club. The club now leases the estate from Crump's grandson Walter, who runs a marina in Sausalito.

Dutcher told me that Crump was a well-known surgeon who practiced in New York City. Built of cobblestones, the castle accommodated a T.B. sanitorium on 380 acres with a hospital, swimming pool, and nurses' quarters, all established by Crump.

I asked Dutcher about one yarn circulating in Duffy's Mountain Tavern (a couple of miles from the Castle as the crow flies) that the nurses served as Crump's harem. According to old-timers in Bushnellsville and Deep Notch, wild orgies were common on the remote estate, aided and abetted by the febrile patients. The wanton nurses frolicked under a harvest moon as the Teutonic surgeon wolfed down his knockwurst and then, bellowing, buried himself in that ministering, accommodating flesh. When I'd first heard it, this tale captured my imagination. The image was irresistible, as enduring as the beard graying on Van Winkle's chin.

Walter dispelled these rumors. He visited the estate often as a child and said that Crump never even ran a sanitorium. The castle was the centerpiece of a 387-acre dairy farm, built in 1902. Doc Crump, like his father before him (not German, but English and a stone mason) was a freethinker and an abolitionist. Walter said Crump was one of the three or four most famous surgeons in the United States in his day, a gynecological pioneer.

Walter described Crump, "He was 5'7" with a Vandyke mustache. A little chubby, portly. He wore a morning suit, stick pins in his tie, a gold watch. He looked like an Edwardian gentleman. He was a great orator, a dynamo. Slept three hours a night. When we'd go to the farm he'd recite poetry as he drove. He called his place the 'Castle in the Clouds.' "

When I told Walter about the legends that the Castle spawned, he just laughed. "I don't think his wife Eudora would have gone for that. My grandfather was no saint but he wouldn't have had time. He was a very serious, hard-working man."

Crump the freethinker. Crump the abolitionist. Crump the original gynecologist. It's easy to see today why an erotic aura clings to the Castle. Even though the gun club uses the place during hunting season and regularly patrols the premises, teenagers (like Witte's kids) use the grounds and dilapidated buildings for rights of passage.

The day was getting on. I left Nancy Smith and set out for the Castle itself. Cutting through extensive new development I followed Upper Birch Creek Road to where the houses ended and pavement turned to dirt. I was running close to the corner of Delaware, Greene, and Ulster Counties. I rounded a sharp turn spanning a gulch, and the road pursed. Recent tire tracks bit into the soft ground. I was on the saddle between Halcott and Rose Mountains. The road was rough but passable. My directions were vague. I parked three quarters of a mile past the gulch and proceeded on foot, following an abandoned road into the woods. I thought I might be following the Witte kids' tracks, which ended in a tangle of raspberry bushes. Crushed Budweiser cans littered the grass. I wondered how many girls had lost their virginity in these abandoned fields.

The raspberries were tart. I plucked the furry crimson nubs from their clasps. After the first few strays, I waited for a handful and then gobbled. I'd had nothing to eat or drink since breakfast. I was having a fine time but wasn't getting any closer to the Castle. Crossing a small stream, I picked my way through discarded tires. Stone foundations submerged in enveloping underbrush. The path I followed peaked then leveled. I halted, perched myself on a stone, and cracked Mrs. Smith's book. She recounted the Kingston stage, when Pine Hill was the terminus and the big hill checked the run. Stages left

Kingston in the morning, hit Pine Hill midday and returned by evening. The driver must have had a hell of a job. Route 28 was a plank road but ten miles an hour was still a pretty good pace.

Putting the book aside I checked my maps. I was a mile and a thousand feet from the summit of Halcott. I felt like climbing, but turned around. Wading through the berry patch, I noticed yet another abandoned road aiming toward a brightening in the woods above. Instinct told me I was on a wild goose chase. But off I went, pausing often to savor the berries that thrived along the grassy embankments.

The walking was fine. I swung through a highland of laurel, hardwood, and lush fern. Although I was only a mile or two from the nearest thoroughfare, the world seemed very far away. I had the forest to myself. The path I walked might have been built by tanners or farmers. Now the occasional hunter uses it to stalk rabbit, turkey, deer, and bear. As I continued upward, the quest for the Castle dwindled. The fairyland turrets and pennants grew dimmer, replaced by the forest and a forgotten path to nowhere. The road curved through basins and shoals of ferns. Rhythmically striding, I put thought to sleep.

A woodpecker's knock, knock, knock brought the Castle back. Nurses materialized, physical and unabashed. They were wrapped in pennants. They wore turrets for hats. They skipped through the tall grass gathering berries. They gracefully dove into Crump's pool, built with stones dragged from the Esopus by oxen. I could see two long rows of beds set up in the Castle hall. They slept above the sheets unclothed. I heard their tranquil breathing, the satin whisper of their moving limbs.

Again inspired, I strode back to my car. I thought I'd venture in another direction before giving up the Castle search. I tromped down the road toward Bushnellsville. Soon a gate appeared; beyond, a level driveway. Eureka!

I had found it. I followed the driveway to a blasted barn with wrought-iron insets and advanced to the caretaker's cottage, which now serves as the gun club's lodge. It was relatively intact, but behind the lodge were ruins.

There wasn't much to see—remnants of cobblestone walls; vestiges of the original frame. I revisited the barn and poached more berries, surprised that they'd been spared by the birds. Then I admired the view from the lodge porch while the light mellowed and the day cooled.

I skimmed the ridge lines with binoculars and settled down to study some Emerson before going back to the car. Berries not withstanding, my stomach growled. I had also developed a terrific thirst. Here are some of the quotes from the essay "Self-Reliance," which I served up for sustenance:

> In every work of genius we recognize our own rejected thoughts; they come back to us with a certain alienated majesty.

> What have I to do with the sacredness of traditions, if I live wholly from within?

> My book should smell of pines and resound with the hum of insects. The swallow over my window should interweave that thread of straw he carries in his bill into my web also. We pass for what we are.

Alienated majesty! Living wholly from within! My book of pines and insect hum! Emerson, as always, was refreshing (but does he go on!). After twenty pages of sermonizing and admonition, my attention wandered. I imagined Crump reciting poetry and summoned the nurses.

But only birds rustled in the undergrowth; they flicked from branch to branch. A large animal shifted in the woods and started to move slowly but steadily, perhaps fifty yards from where I sat. I put Emerson down. Stalking to the top of a stone wall I peered into the forest's depths but couldn't see what lurked. Was it deer or bear? Or something else? One could always hope—or fear.

I felt night coming a shade more quickly than it had only weeks before. The sky was dense, cloudless, bluer than blue. I glanced at the barn, a spooky wreck. Did spirits haunt? Were nurses luscious half a century dead? I zipped up the day pack and made for the car. I dined in Pine Hill as dusk filled the valleys and a strange light lingered on the peaks above.

Several weeks after my ramble to the Castle, Walter sent me a package of Xeroxed material. Enclosed I found an admirer's description of Crump's place during its heyday:

There is the charming old farmhouse with its outlying buildings; the stone milk house, the woodshed, the tool-house, the various houses for poultry—the great barn with stone basement for horses and cattle and roomy upper part for haymows, workshops, harness and grain room—the stone Castle guest house, 25 × 70, three stories high, with every story on the ground floor, by building on a side hill. The classic Lichen Lodge of selected water-worn boulders with great overhanging green tiled roof, and Castle-like extension to the north. The long pergola just south of the great sloping retaining wall. The beautiful stone swimming pool in a sunken garden—the orchards—the many stone walls—the great sloping pastures—the turbulent mountain streams—above all, the quiet and the cool velvety air, ever inviting one meditation, to quickened thought and to well-earned rest.

It must have indeed been an impressive place! Crump hired thirty-five locals, full-time, to help with construction. He raided mansions on Fifth Avenue (demolished to make way for skyscrapers) for stained glass, detailing, and furniture.

Walter had also included a packet of Crump's abolitionist writings, including a sonnet titled "The Song of the Soul," a paean of praise "for our most alien race, the Negro." Walter told me that Crump, like the pied piper, led a convoy of N.A.A.C.P. bigwigs, dressed to the hilt, to vacation at the Castle. Walter chuckled at the thought of them rolling in stately fashion through Shandaken. No wonder Crump spawned legends! Another enclosure: an elegiac essay in which Crump recounts how John Burroughs (in the last year of his life) dragged the good doctor out one wet morning to hunt a woodchuck that had been raiding the garden. Burroughs gets a shot but misses. Crump says:

"Mr. Burroughs, you should rest more and jot down your wonderful thoughts.... This woodchuck game is a strenuous one."

"Yes," Burroughs answered. "But one must have a change and incidents to prime the pump of the intellect."

I loved the notion of Burroughs roused to his last great thoughts by blasting a bothersome woodchuck!

After mulling it over, I had a nagging suspicion that during my initial foray I'd overlooked the Castle remains. In the material Walter had sent were aerial photos of the estate. The Castle and Crump's pagoda-style residence seemed to be beyond the gun club lodge, in an area I hadn't explored. So I set out for Pine Hill, Upper Birch Creek Road, and the Castle once again.

I was not disappointed. The Castle was still standing, upslope from the lodge, hidden in entangling forest. It was a pre-Raphaelite ruin: all the windows broken; the elaborate wrought-iron doors and railings rusted. I entered, picking my way with care, shards of glass cracking under my boots. A magnificence endured in the grim stone shell. I marvelled at the energy and imagination that had created such a place.

I climbed the spiral staircase and lounged on a window ledge in the great hall. Damp from recent heavy rain permeated the crumbling concrete. The stone walls sweated. Cool currents of air passed through the long, dark room.

I thought of Crump and felt a fierce affinity with this man who had so obviously been a dreamer and was just as obviously rooted in the earth. I wondered what he would have thought sitting where I sat then, surveying the ravages of his creation. I heard water pouring off the mountainside, a hammer pounding down Bushnellsville way, the wind blowing through the trees. I traced the drip, drip, drip coming off the ceiling, like tears or falling stars.

Aphorisms and axioms were spelled out in small squares of white tile set into the Castle fireplaces, window sills, and entryway floors. Here are three of my favorites:

> Whoever you are,
> Whatever you believe,
> You are welcome here.

> The world is my country,
> To do good, my religion.

Linger here amid the beautiful foolishness of things.

THE SUSQUEHANNA
TURNPIKE RAMBLE

"MY FATHER TOLD ME campfires burned on Gun Hill at night as far as the eye could see. Settlers going west," said Earl C. Smith, age ninety-three. Smith's forbearers, however, did not go west. They settled down the road in Durham, and Smith was a Catskill man. He lived with daughter and son-in-law, Anne and Bill Thorpe, in what was once one of the Susquehanna Turnpike's many inns.

For much of the nineteenth century, the turnpike stretched from Catskill to Unadilla, bridging the Hudson and Susquehanna River Valleys. Inns like the Thorpes's sprang up to accommodate heavy traffic. At its height, the turnpike handled over a thousand wagons a day.

Verona Fleurent, curator of the Durham Center Museum which houses Turnpike memorabilia, said that after the Revolutionary War, western New York was viewed as the new frontier. The turnpike attracted Connecticut veterans who wanted to make a new start. It was no free ride. Built for profit, its tolls in 1800 included: eight cents for each score of sheep and hogs; twenty cents for each score of horses and mules; five cents for a horse and rider; twelve-and-a-half cents for sulkey, cart, or chaise with one horse; and twenty-five cents for chariot, coach, choachee, or phaeton. Doctors and ministers were exempt from tolls. So were people going to funerals or to church. The Durham area was originally Presbyterian, then Methodist. There were high fines for gate crashing. Most of the traffic was English stock.

In Greene County, the turnpike operated from 1800 to 1902, making it the longest lived toll road in this country's history. In 1973 its Greene County section was added to the National Register of Historic Places. Fleurent said that as late as 1850 wagons were backed up from Catskill to Leeds, a distance of several miles, waiting to unload goods shipped down the Hudson to feed the big city.

Today the turnpike is difficult to follow, even with the Historic Places designation. Most people along its route are oblivious to its historical significance. It is poorly marked, reclusive, and skittish—or so I found when I drove it from Cairo to Unadilla on July 1.

Possessing a sketchy map of the turnpike's course, I picked it up heading toward East Durham on Route 145. Like Route 32 to the south, Route 145 is dregs: a wasteland of go-carts, miniature golf, snack bars, taverns, and chintzy motels. Leprechauns and shamrocks beckoned on road houses and bungalow complexes with names like Killarney and O'Neil. Billboards advertised Seamus McKeague singing that night somewhere in the wee country.

With the Fourth of July fast approaching, trailer and hostelry alike had hoisted American flags. Second-hand goods were strewn by the roadside. Everywhere there was something to buy. The holiday, like all other American holidays, seemed geared for commerce.

The rural poverty of this northern tier of the Catskills

had a distinctly different texture than its southern counter-part. In the south, poverty has an Appalachian, panhandle feel—as though industry had come and gone, or the land had become worn and worthless. Another characteristic of southern Catskill poverty is that it co-exists alongside bastions of privilege, such as fishing clubs of the upper Beaverkill and the thousands of acres Laurence Rockefeller owns. In this part of the northern tier the indigence came from an overflow of rinky-dink operations, most of them catering to the lower-middle-class.

The whole schmeer bordered on bankruptcy. Entering East Durham, I noted "for sale" signs on most houses. I pulled over to check out a vintage Cadillac hearse. A plaque on its driver's window read "asking $2,500 but will consider a Virgo Intruder Motorcycle, etc., etc. trade." Why etc., etc.? The seller certainly had specific ideas about transport.

Parked in front of an antique-crafts shop was a black Amish Lancaster wagon with original lights and brakes to conform to Pennsylvania state law. Inside, a carved Amish couple stared out with frozen faces at the passing traffic. "I am for sale," ended the explanatory placard. Large carvings of a rotund Santa, tomahawk wielding Indian, buckskin coonhat pioneer, and owl completed the open-air diorama.

Peggy Evans said handwritten missives stapled to telephone polls pleading "Save East Durham and Corn-wallville" opposed an impending mega-dump. (Originally from County Limerick, Evans runs an East Durham road-side shop. Her husband—a large man with a florid, liver-spotted face—would have nothing to do with me. She, on the other hand—cheerful, frumpy, and gnomish—was full of information. The resorts I had passed catered to eastern-seaboard Irish who came here instead of vacation-ing in the old country. Jigs and reels highlighted May's Irish Festival, which drew 40,000.) North of East Durham

I sped past the ominous Stiefel Research Institute. The Catskills tapered to rolling hills. "ZOOM FLUME" signs sprouted by the wayside every few miles; the "flume" turned out to be waterslide of prodigious proportions. I was tempted, but Unadilla beckoned.

Planning the trip, I had known that I was in for a four-county junket. I hadn't, however, anticipated crossing the Albany County line. Befuddled, I turned around at "Rustic Cabin, Home of the Funseekers." At Route 22, a historical marker proclaimed: "Susquehanna Turnpike, Incorporated 1800, Placed on the National Register of Historic Places, January 2, 1974." By its side stood the Susquehanna United Methodist Church. I had found it! The turnpike did, indeed, exist. Excited, I took photos of the church, feeling as though I was on to something. With a sense of mission I headed west out of Durham up the pike's one steep grade. With my four cylinders firing neatly, I imagined oxen straining up the rise—everyone out, and the men bending their backs, pushing from behind.

According to the 1975 Catskill Center Susquehanna Turnpike survey undertaken by Richard Kathmann, then curator of the Old Mill Museum in East Meredith, the turnpike was capitalized by Catskill landowners and local businessmen for $12,000 at $20 a share. The investors made money from selling land and supplying travelers, as well as from tolls. Because of indirect revenues, it's impossible to calculate shareholder profits. After the 1820 advent of the Erie Canal, sections of the turnpike collapsed. Towns and counties took over maintenance.

Kathmann now lives in New Hampshire, having recently left the Shaker Village Museum after ten years as director. He said the survey's impulse "was to document what was left of the Catskills's historical resources. Which, it turned out, were not as fragile as they first seemed." The survey concentrated on cataloging inns and residences.

It was part of the general bicentennial preoccupation with history.

A turnpike is a toll road, by definition. The *Oxford English Dictionary* says that use of the word originated in the fifteenth century. It denoted, then, a line of defense—a bristled ditch or spiked barrier. For the next three centuries the word often appeared as "turne pyke." In 1745 came the first known mention of turnpikes as toll roads; and the concept has persisted. Kathmann writes that by 1820, New York State's entire breadth and width was connected by toll roads.

The country west of Durham was exquisite. To one side the dramatic line of the Catskills's eastern escarpment swept south. North were rolling hills, barns, and high pasture. Pavement turned to dirt. I stopped after driving several miles, sure that I had somehow missed my turn, thrown off by a sign that said Durham Road. My doubts were laid to rest when I came to the Thorpe place.

Cousins Charlotte and Edwin Hitchcock were chatting with the Thorpes on their wide front lawn. Anne Thorpe threw up her hands in delight when told that I was not only on the turnpike, I was looking at an original turnpike inn—and curse the town board that had put up the Durham Road sign!

Anne said that an interview would rouse her father, and I was invited inside. Once I'd been seated with notepad poised, she bustled off to fetch Mr. Smith and returned with several books, one by Beatrice Mattice, the others by the Atkinsons (a former drama critic for the *New York Times* and a novelist.) Smith made his entrance slowly. A tall man, he ducked under the inn's low ceilings and propped himself in a high-back chair before a folding table littered with newspapers and a game of solitaire set out in bold-faced cards.

"My great-grandfather sold lumber at $18 a 1000 feet," he reminisced. "He worked the mill at night when he couldn't work the land. His first purchase payday was a ten-gallon keg of liquor."

"What kind of liquor?" I asked.

"Anything would make him drink," scoffed Smith, pleased with the set-up.

He talked about drovers, some of whom were turkey drivers (the Catskill equivalent of cowboys). We all remarked, What a strange way to make a living! And wasn't it a shame the word, along with the trade, had disappeared. Smith also talked pitch tar. Not pine resin set up hard, but the sticky black paste drovers brewed in holes. For what? Your guess is as good as mine. I posed Smith for his "photo op" under a wonderful portrait of a middle-aged woman with an elongated nose, bulging eyes, and an expression of surpassing sourness.

"It's been said Thorpe women *all* look like that after fifty," said Bill—and almost immediately tried to retract the statement.

Anne had been chattering, goading the men on and flipping through her books. She handed over Oriana Atkinson's *Big Eyes*. It began: "There was in Connecticut a man named Crown, along about 1790. And Crown, because of undesirable neighbors, or family troubles or simply because of a wish for solitude or new country, stuck a sprig of lilac in the ribbon of his old hat, mounted his horse and rode North and West."

With close to a hundred miles to cover before sundown I figured I'd better giddy-up. Anne promised to Xerox and mail me the turnpike chapter in Mattice's book, *They Walked These Hills Before Me, An Early History of the Town of Conesville*.

Manorkill and Conesville passed in a blur. At the Gilboa Reservoir spillway, I broke the drive and gazed at the turbid water searching for fish. When I looked up, the sky had receded. My mind turned blank contemplating all the dull, blazing space. I wanted to fish, but there was nothing rising. The wind would have blown my fly to Buffalo.

Charles Olson, in *Call Me Ishmael, A Study of Melville,* writes:

> I take SPACE to be the central fact to man born in America, from Folsom cave to now. I spell it large because it comes large here. Large, and without mercy...a harshness we still perpetuate, a sun like a tomahawk, small earthquakes but big tornadoes and hurrikans, a river north and south in the middle of the land running out the blood...Americans still fancy themselves democrats. But their triumphs are of the machine. It is the only master of space the average person ever knows, oxwheel to piston, muscle to jet. It gives trajectory...Like Ahab, American, one aim: lordship over nature.

Trajectory, the arc that gives life shape and meaning—is that what the Susquehanna settlers thought? Were they dazzled by the continent spread out before them? How did they envision the Mississippi and the plains beyond? It's hard to believe that they were as bereft of ideology as Olson suggests. Many of these men had laid down their lives for independence, inalienable rights, and economic control.

As I traced the route so many had traveled before me, I hoped to conjure what had driven those settlers to the "land beyond the Blue Mountains." I wanted to get inside their heads and see what they saw as they entered this new country. I hoped to mimic the inclination of the early surveyor's eye (unveil the trajectory) as he scoped the turnpike's path. But in Gilboa I was lost again. The reservoir had disrupted the valley's natural course. The road kinked south, and I found myself heading toward Prattsville.

Traveling Route 23 from Prattsville to Stamford was a breeze, but there was nothing to indicate whether I was on or off the pike. I made a leap of faith and drove blithely on. In Stamford I stretched my legs, trudging up a back road past Victorian mansions to a forgotten mill site on the Delaware's headwaters.

Brown water seethed in a small pond littered with debris: broken bottles, old tires, footwear of all descriptions, and a plastic sled. I have generally found the Delaware a drainage ditch for cow manure and fertilizer. The foulness at its source came as no surprise. Mosquitos were thick.

South of Stamford I was lost again—deep in the never-never land around Kortright. After trundling aimlessly for the better part of an hour I beheld the single word "TURNPIKE" emblazoned on a small green sign. I turned up a dirt road. At the first farm I pulled over. Farmer Kenyon ("JESUS IS LORD" freshly painted on one of his outbuildings) came to his front door in overalls. A tight-lipped man, he looked consumed by worries and work. Kenyon knew the road as the Catskill Turnpike.

Barbecuing with his buddies behind the parsonage a couple of miles further along, Danny Haines agreed. Haines—beer in one hand, spatula in the other—looked like he didn't have a care in the world. He said that name change from Susquehanna to Catskill made sense since the turnpike's terminus in Unadilla was close. His big dog Boo had dragged a dead woodchuck to the parsonage lawn and shook the reeking carcass with delight. As we talked, Boo bounded over and coated me with slobber of dead woodchuck. Haines assured me that I was only half an hour away from my journey's end. For several miles I followed the wayward turnpike like a bloodhound

on a felon's scent. But, inevitably, somewhere in Meredith
I went wrong. I remembered an unlikely looking turnoff
marked by a sprawling white clapboard of colonial mein.
That convinced me. Susquehanna-style inns, road houses,
and residences—not present roads—were the true clues
to the old pike's route.

After a forty-minute detour to Delhi I reclaimed the
turnpike east of Treadwell. I knew I was on track again
by the colonial houses dotting the roadside and the way
the road followed the river valley with a gentle grade. I
finally rolled into Unadilla, which was pretty and western.
The nearly comatose teenager who took my gas money
knew nothing about turnpikes. He wore a black, heavy-
metal t-shirt and had a python tattooed on his arm—a
sinister touch in what seemed a peaceful, backwater town.

I found a condemned bridge where I sat perched over
the Susquehanna—wide, muddy, and fast—on a skeleton
of rusted girders. Caddis hatched off the river. Swooping
black birds took them in midair. One bird swiped a caddis
with its beak but failed to nab it. The caddis plummeted
downward. Just as it was about to hit the water, a trout
leapt and snagged it. That caddis' number was up.

I wondered if the Connecticut boys went west because
they believed, as we have come to believe, that anything
is possible, the opportunities endless. Was it (to use
Olson's terms) "lordship over nature" that these settlers
were after? Were they Ahabs locked in mortal combat with
nature in all its implacable power?

I think not. As I sat above the swift-moving Susquehanna I pictured them coming into Unadilla, tentative and
tired from the road. The land beyond the blue mountains
must have seemed far from home. They carried few
belongings and little money. Others settled in the Finger
Lakes, and some continued to the Ohio Valley. Some took
the trajectory to its end and landed in Oregon and Califor-
nia. They were stopped only by the sea. But somehow

(as Olson has said) in their mind's eye they were always looking beyond the Pacific. Since Columbus's time that projection has been lodged in all of us.

I choose to see them as patient rather than obsessed. They coaxed forth rather than blindly pursued, driven by rural fictions of clever accommodations and modest returns.

The light in Unadilla softened. Drawn by another fundamental American urge, part of me wanted to rig a raft and ride the Susquehanna's swift current south and west. Instead I drove north to Oneonta, then turned east on Route 28. Darkness fell. In a Delhi seafood restaurant I dined on broiled fisherman's platter. The world-weary waitress, blue bruises under her eyes, moved with excruciating slowness. The food was bad. A hundred miles of hard driving and I was home.

DEEP INTO WESTKILL

1: APPROACH

IT WAS LATE AT NIGHT when I first entered Westkill Valley. A friend and I drove up the narrow road that worked its way like a needle to the end of the long box canyon. It was the middle of May. The night had been mild in Woodstock, lilac fragrance filling the air. But not in Westkill. The trees were still in tight bud, and the faint wind carried the cool scent of ground newly thawed. Nearing the valley's top, five porcupines rolled off the road in quick succession; deer hurtled across our headlights; small eyes flashed in the forest and were gone.

We parked the truck at the Spruceton trail head. Animal odor was rife: the smell of warming hide; old fur ready to shed. I stood in the middle of a field, then walked by moonlight to a fast-flowing stream. The full moon hung like a pendulum over the jagged ridgeline of Westkill Mountain, a glimmering carpet across the water at my feet.

My friend stood beside me—shuffling, sighing, still wanting to talk. The previous spring, he had fallen in love while camping a quarter of a mile upstream. The couple consummated their relationship in a tent next to the woman's two sleeping children. Soon after, she left her husband. That spring, he was completely enamored. Now she left him cold.

I stood watching the moon through sticks chattering in the breeze. Winter chill seeped from the rushing stream into my bones, and the witching hour waned. I felt numb inside. We returned to the truck and drove home to Woodstock through Deep Notch.

2: UNCLE HARRY

I could have lain on the flat rock and basked in the sun all day. Five years earlier I would have, without question. I'd been comtemplating the waterfall at the head of Platteclove—falling without pause, ceaselessly dropping, but to my eye oddly static. I thought of the Taoist precept: The waterfall fills the pool above as well as below. For obscure and (Taoistically) insidious reasons, I pulled myself together, ducked back into the car, and proceeded up the old Tannersville highway into the Schoharie Valley. I was going back to Westkill by day.

In Elka Park, dogwoods flecked the forest with mother-of-pearl. A profusion of apple and cherry bloomed, reminiscent of the days when settling in the Catskills meant planting orchards. The backside of the Twin-Indian Head range rose sharply against the blue sky and cut a straight line westward. I passed the Eggery Inn, spruced-up and ready for summer, and Cold Springs Hotel, dilapidated and haunted, a remnant of the past.

Pockets of artificial snow clung to Hunter's ski slopes. The wide swaths of clear-cut trails looked useless and forlorn. Nose in the air, a possum trotted across the highway as I drove slowly through the center of town.

West of Hunter, the tacky-resort, boom-bust feel of the

Palenville-Tannersville-Hunter nexus shifted; in its place were farms and rolling fields. I felt that timelessness which is time, flowing like water falling in the falls, steady yet static. The Schoharie Creek ran by the side of the road, muddy with the previous night's rain. Good trout fishing this time of year.

In Lexington, I bought a quart of grapefruit juice, sat in the car, and looked out over the last year's corn stubble. An old man in a blue imitation-down vest, leaning heavily on a cane, came limping toward me across the lot.

"Good day to you!" he hollered.

"Good day to you!"

He propped himself against the car's side and peered at me sideways. "I know you from someplace. You look familiar. You're from around here. Am I right?"

I told him I was from Woodstock.

"You know Ron Merians? I know Ron Merians. I worked for him washing dishes in the Joyous Lake."

I told him that I had washed dishes there, too, when I was sixteen.

"That's where I knowed you from," he beamed. I asked his name.

"Everyone calls me Uncle Harry!"

That jogged my memory. This was the same Uncle Harry who had trained me as a dishwasher, a man about whom I used to rhapsodize to my friends. Harry was deft. He was expert. He was impervious to the pain of scalding dishwater. Harry could pick plates out of the dish-pans and loft them into the stainless steel bubble-bath sinks across the small washroom without breaking a one; and he had a repertoire of saucy responses to the panicky, short-skirted waitresses that always seemed to be snapping for clean cups.

And here was Harry in the flesh, seventeen years later, leaning through the window of my car and going on about how he used to drive fifty miles there and fifty miles back and get up at four every morning and not get home until midnight; and about his two strokes and his son dying of cancer, hospital bills stripping the savings ("but what the hell, money was no object, we had to do what was right"). Harry wanted to go for a ride "up Westkill way."

"Think you're up for climbing a mountain?" I asked.

"I climbed up all over these mountains." He stiffly motioned toward the lower reaches of Packsaddle, Pine Island, and Evergreen Mountains. "When I was younger." He grinned his boyish grin.

"You married?" he asked. I nodded. "But you're like me, only married when you're home!" Pleased with his sally, he patted my arm and brayed. Pointing across the road to the gray thirteen-room house he had owned with his wife for forty years, he made me promise to come back.

"You promise to come back? I can count on it?" I promised and left.

3: VALLEY FOLK

A couple of weeks later, back in Westkill, I dropped in on Floyd and Lloyd Kirk. Floyd was born fifteen minutes after Lloyd in a farm midway up the Valley. The Kirk brothers are eighty-seven years old. In 1971, they sold the family homestead and moved to a ramshackle trailer sitting on an acre of immaculate lawn. They have a satellite dish. Inside the trailer are two cots, placed side by side and covered with rough wool blankets. The odor inside the trailer was rank.

Both men were fading but still rather valiantly functional. Lloyd said "I don't remember much," when I asked for information. Leaning on an aluminum ski pole, he crept across the lawn and gassed up a tractor-mower in slow motion. Floyd sat on one of the cots and told me that his grandfather had come to the valley in 1831, built the first log cabin in Spruceton, and sired eleven children by two wives.

The brothers both chewed massive wads of rough-cut tobacco, the remains of which, like sodden golf balls, littered the lawn and nestled in various makeshift receptacles about the trailer. As Floyd talked, a stream of tobacco juice ran down a well-worn crinkle to the right side of his mouth; he wiped it away in an unconscious movement with a handkerchief taken from the front pocket of his baggy green pants.

Floyd wanted to go for a ride up to the old homestead ("helps limber me up"). He fetched a worn cap to cover his white wisps. Lloyd stiffly mounted the mower as we drove away.

Floyd pointed to houses he had built as we drove up the valley, places of dead friends and neighbors. "No one left here," he said.

Midway to Spruceton, we crossed a rickety bridge over the Westkill Stream. The Kirk homestead is now Susita Farms. A young woman came bumping toward us in a pickup. Her name was Glenda Lauten, Dr. Uriel Adar's caretaker. Adar, an Israeli orthopedic surgeon who comes up weekends, had recently turned Susita into a breeding farm for thoroughbreds. Lauten, completely open and relaxed, showed me around the stables. Several sable-brown mares were penned with their foals.

I jumped in her pickup, and we went to inspect more of Adar's stock corralled in the back forty. Floyd stayed by the barn and had himself "a look around." At the top of Adar's spread, I could see into Ulster County through the notch between North Dome and Westkill Mountains. The sky turned black; then it started to pour. On the way down the mountain, Lauten pointed out where Floyd and Lloyd had stockpiled hundreds of junked cars. When Adar bought the property, he buried them all.

We met Floyd back in the barn. Lauten offere to explain some of the techniques of thoroughbred breeding. She took Cricket, a brown and white "teaser" pony, from his stall. Cricket, she said, tells her if the mares are in heat. She walked Cricket over to Sunnydots, a ten-year-old mare. Sunnydots stuck her muzzle through the bars of her stall. Cricket began to sniff and pant. The mare excitedly snorted, velvet muzzle quivering, big teeth bared, lips snarling. Cricket stomped.

"Talk, Cricket! Talk!" urged Lauten. The pony whinnied and huffed, hyperventilating, his muzzle straining through the bars. Lauten said that if a mare is in heat she will turn, present her posterior to the male, and lift her tail.

"Piss'll start to fly," Floyd interjected.

Both mares in the barn were between heat and foal. They gave the pony an ambivalent response. A pony is used to tease because even if he gets loose he's too small to mount. Lauten (perhaps to placate me) said she plans to breed Cricket eventually and give him a taste of the real thing.

I dropped Floyd home and idled back up the valley. Past Susita Farms, I stopped at Schwarzenegger's Sunshine Valley House, Karl and Dolores proprietors. Dolores sat me down in a restaurant nook lined with photos from Conan movies. It turned out that Arnold Schwarzenegger is Karl's nephew and comes to Westkill periodically.

"He's been skiing at Hunter and running on the road," said Karl proudly.

I took the couple's photo in the celebrity nook, and then set up a solo shot of Karl in front of a stuffed bobcat he had shot years ago in Huntersfield Mountain.

4: MOUNTAIN LIONS

Researching an article on forest rangers, I had occasion to talk to Rick Dearstyne, the ranger who covers the

Westkill Valley. I asked him if he saw much wildlife in his area. After the usual stories of bear and such, he paused. Then he said he had seen a mountain lion the previous summer. He told me the following story.

Two months after he had moved from Long Island to the Catskills he was bushwhacking off Balsam Mountain toward his cabin on Spruceton Road. It was late June, just after dusk.

"I was in a hurry to get back. I was doing everything I always tell everyone not to do—I was in the woods without a light, without a compass."

He heard a growl.

"It stopped me in my tracks. I denied it to myself. It had a full-throated voice and sounded like one hell of a bobcat."

Dearstyne started moving again. Immediately came another growl. He whistled for Max, his 140-pound Rottweiler. As Max came to his side, another growl sounded close in the night woods.

"It was an eerie feeling in the dark. I felt it could see me and hear me and I couldn't see it. I didn't want Max to tangle with it. I wanted to get him back down to the house."

Still not sure what he had heard, Dearstyne came home the next day around 6:30; his wife was running toward their house. She had been walking Max down by the Westkill Stream and saw a big cat slinking through the tall grass less than a hundred yards away. Dearstyne went down to the stream and found paw prints in the mud that were "obviously much too big for a bobcat." That evening he tracked the lion up the south side of the valley.

"I found where it had killed a deer. I nearly stumbled on the kill. I couldn't see it but I could smell it. The cat had dragged the kill under a rock ledge and covered it." He disturbed the kill: "I kicked it. Brushed it over."

The next morning he was up before dawn and staked out the kill. Using binoculars, at sun-up he watched the cat prowl a wide circle around the kill site. He confirmed it was indeed a mountain lion and decided to leave it alone.

"It made my 140-pound Rottweiler look tiny. It was the color of Long Island sand with a *very* long tail."

One other person in the valley saw the mountain lion: twelve-year-old Tom Graff, who was out hiking with a friend. "I saw a bright flash. Something running, big as a deer but yellow. It ran up a tree."

Graff said he could see the cougar's paws wrapped around the trunk, claws sunk into the bark. He said he felt excited, elated, but "freaked out." He walked until he was out of the lion's sight and then took off down the mountain.

No one believed him when he said he had seen what looked like a mountain lion run up a tree. That is, until Dearstyne came by a couple of days later and confirmed the story. The valley folk heard the beast growling at dusk for ten days following, but no one caught sight of it again.

Dearstyne said he knows for a fact that the DEC had released four mated pairs of mountain lions eight years before into the northern Catskills. He also said that he'd heard one pair were released in Spruceton: "The DEC is closed-mouthed about it. They'll deny it through their teeth to the public."

5: THE HIKE

In early June, when I hiked Westkill Mountain (and walked down memory lane with Uncle Harry), I was still blissfully unaware that a mountain lion might cross my path. I parked opposite Dearstyne's cabin beside a souped-up sky-blue Chevy Malibu with ultraviolet windows.

Dangling from the rearview mirror were two oversized black dice with white dots.

I strapped on my daypack and headed up the old Westkill-Hunter road. A young couple sunbathed on the stone pilings of an old bridge. The woman stood; she wore a flashy-red, one-piece bathing suit, zipped in front. The man lounged in cutoffs.

Along the old road, small clearings were marked by central fire circles. Half a mile in, the trail frayed: one fork to Hunter's summit; another to Mink Hollow; the third to the top of Westkill Mountain—my destination.

Crews hadn't touched the trail since winter. Spring storms had driven dead limbs off the trees and dropped deadfalls. I tromped along, knowing I had a stiff climb ahead, savoring the task.

Pain is part of every spiritual pursuit, and to commune with nature involves certain necessary rites of purification (or so I told myself). Walking up mountains for me is a form of meditation: the slow rhythm of steps; the deep, labored breathing; the heavy heartbeat.

Communion with nature is the most authentic form of spiritual pursuit. All else is elaboration, embroidery. Around me the new forest danced in the early afternoon breeze. Basswood bloomed. I climbed and climbed, sweating out toxins, cleaning the pores, letting thought-loops idle and spin, going deep into myself and reemerging, picking my steps up rock and scree, over fallen branches and deadfalls, treading packed earth through a tunnel of leaves.

I broke the hike, stopping in the middle of a particularly steep section of trail. Slumped on a big stone, I opened my grapefruit juice and drank. The arm tipping the juice into my mouth (like Dr. Strangelove) suddenly had a mind of its own; before I knew what I was about, I was guzzling the tart nectar with complete abandon. I sat panting in a daze.

Fat flies buzzed, yellow leaf-marks on their bulbous ebony bottoms. I felt languorous and drowsy. A cool breeze touched the forest. Pulling myself together, I continued the climb. The basswood flower had a heavy scent. I remembered Nelson Shultis telling me that basswood pollen makes delicious honey. "That's some delicious honey," he had said.

I came to what looked like a spring (but turned out to be a semi-underground tricklet). I shed my pack, dropped to my knees in the mud and loose stone, sank my head among the roots, and slurped. High, in balsam now, the trail crested a false summit. It snaked along the long horizontal of Westkill's ridgeline, bearing west. The mossy ground was spongy with boxspring roots and fiddlehead fern. I plucked one and ambled along with my chew.

Cries bayed in the woods behind me. Small hairs rose on the nape of my neck: the sound was like a beast in pain. I stealthily retraced my steps. After perhaps twenty paces, I saw a couple deliriously coupling in the ferns and new green, her legs arched over his back, his blond head buried in her breasts. She cried and moaned, the sound coming from deep inside her, like a primal release. They were a stone's throw from where I stood. I think he felt my presence because his head rose. As our eyes were about to meet I wheeled away, shaken.

As I staggered uptrail she started to sob. Was she in trouble? There was not another soul for miles around. I checked myself and started to retrace my steps. Were those cries of pain? I saw her legs around his back. I hesitated and then went on.

Through the dense mesh of balsam, cirrus clawed the sky. A stiff wind pressed from the northwest. It turned cold. I sprawled on the edge of a spectacular lookout, goggling at the view from Jewitt to Bellayre. Scanning the ridge of Westkill Mountain with my binoculars, I remembered the pine woods behind Peter Pan Farm opposite Pam

Copeland's field, where I went to camp the first summer of my adolescence.

My friend, older than me by two years, lured a girl named Lee into the woods and seduced her on a bed of pine needles warmed by the afternoon sun. I watched them at a distance, flushed and fascinated, throat thick, unable to swallow or breathe. He wore white bell-bottom jeans and wire-rim glasses.

"Your turn," he said to me, finished. I remember his voice, full of contempt—a spent, hard, masculine disdain. She lay there, torpid and swollen. He left. I'll never forget her lisp, long hair, and unzipped jeans. I walked over, reached down, and helped her up. We walked back to the camp in silence.

Years later, as I wandered through the mountains, while stooping by hidden mountain pools to drink or dallying in groves, I'd often rise hoping to see a nymph meet my hungry eyes. I searched through the hills, yearning with the full force of my being for that numinous place where the maenads danced. Always, on the edge of hearing, I heard their wet impassioned sighs.

On Westkill Mountain, a few raindrops splattered the lookout stone. A high wind shifted eastward, whipping the windbreaker across my back. It was time to descend. I stopped where I had seen the couple. Only a slight indentation remained in the dead leaves and moss. An opalescent drop clung to a crushed fern.

Given the choice now I would rather see a mountain lion than a nymph. Nymphs are peripheral and always seem—whether on top of Westkill Mountain or in the pinewoods of Zena—elsewhere occupied. The beast, foul with its den, yellow-fanged and growling, is the more genuine form of incarnate spirituality.

Hike finished, I sat in my car near Dearstyne's empty cabin. Slight rain pattered in the quiet woods. Dusk was coming. I flipped on the radio and ran the needle up and down the dial: mostly static. There were shallow tracks in the wet ground. The Malibu was gone.

NIGHTCRAWLERS

I PARKED AT THE three-ton bridge and walked upstream on the fisherman's path. By my side, the headwaters of the Schoharie ran clear and flush. The path faded and reappeared—slight and vaporous, then suddenly strong. Overhead hemlock formed a dense canopy. The path hugged the stream's side then cut back into the forest. The sound of moving water mingled with that of treetops stirring and the phoebe's two-toned call.

It was hot for April. An eerie Bermuda high had settled on the Northeast, the temperature pushing ninety. I thrashed through an undergrowth of alders with new leaves. The river forked in a gravel basin, broken by patches of raised ground. I halted and contemplated the low trees metallically shimmering against an enamel sky. The vista summoned memories of the upper reaches of the Ganges River in the jungles around Rishikesh, where the elephants crossed and the big cats left their prints in the sand. Standing under the blazing sun in Elka Park, I imagined elephants and tigers walking out of the woods

189

at dusk to drink. Not so long ago their precursors did. Mastodons and the sabertooth roamed here at the end of the last ice age 10,000 years ago. I wondered if the attenuation of the monstrous into new forms, relatively benign, is part of life's inherent succession. Was it Konrad Lorenz who said that the insect world is the only place where monsters still exist? An odd anthropomorphic view for a naturalist. Nevertheless, it's undeniable that the gigantism of earlier epochs has given way to smaller, more docile types.

Man included. We are changing, losing hair, teeth, and our senses of hearing and smell. Our species approaches its infantile beginnings. If it survives long enough will our bodies become more graceful, supple, and quick? Athletes keep setting new records. As diets improve, people grow bigger. And think of the related rise in sport as civilizations solidify, calcify, and dissolve. The projection of future delicate men with ballooning cerebra and antennae for hands seems misshapen. Still, the image of the man-child persists. The fetus at the end of *2001* suspended in the uterus of the universe comes to mind. That image's tenacity is one reason that movies like *Alien* or *Gremlins*, which portray man-eating children, are so unsettling: They cast a sinister light on what we see in the tunnel before us.

It's easy to find causes for our obsession with apocalypse. While roasting in the mutagenic heat of that April afternoon, I envisioned the next age dominated by insects—an age that would make all others look tame. Giant wasps swoop out of an infernal sky lancing their hapless prey—paralyzing them to be devoured alive piecemeal. Zillions of locusts blacken the sky. Roaches the size of softballs suck the salt off our skin as we sleep, then move on to nibble at the more tender parts. The infestation complete, all other forms of life squashed, the insects will take to gobbling up each other.

The popular Earth Day cliché—Gaia as Disney—of nature harmoniously balanced (an interwoven, interdependent, symphonic complex euphorically floating in a photosynthetic ambrosia) is simple-minded and regressive. I suspect this idea will spawn growths as ultimately self-serving as Exxon. The popularization of the annual Earth Day event partakes of an underlying optimism rooted in the Enlightenment's Newtonian model of a divinely ordered grand design. The Newtonian model—satellites zipping around the sun in mathematically precise orbits—is the flowering of what Lewis Mumford recognized as the "basis" of modern science: canonical bells simultaneously ringing in thousands of medieval monasteries, calling the faithful to prayer. Strict observance required a regularized device, which inspired the invention of the clock.

On the surface, mysticism and technology are separated by a gulf of distrust and disdain. Probe one step deeper, and they embrace. Science and religion cover the same thing—explanations. Breakthroughs in science are reformational in the same way that religions reform. Both modify authority. They each rest on dogma and sacrilege; both have their cults, lay orders, acolytes, and devotees. The latest being "eco-" (instead of egg) heads in Patagonia jackets, not white smocks. And they have their lapsed souls, one of which I felt like that day.

I plunged back into the forest, the first twitchings of the insect age upon me as I flicked spiders from my neck and scalp and peeled webs from my lips. After nearly an hour of flicking and peeling, I came to a bend in the river. Barbed wire fencing demarcated fields. I stood at the tail end of a brimming pool. Step by step, I worked up its side and assembled my gear. I tied on a small hook and pinched two soft-lead split shots eighteen inches up the line. I yanked to make sure they were tight, then took out my styrofoam bait cup. Its translucent plastic cover had broken, leaving dirt inside my pack. I plucked a crawler from the humid loam. It weakly writhed.

The proprietor of the Rip Van Winkle Bazaar on Main Street in Tannersville had sold me the crawlers earlier that day. Fresh from the fridge, they'd been frisky, madly squirming over his fingers, diving toward envelopment in the dense medium through which they so effortlessly moved. But the heat inside my pack had knocked them out. Taking a medium-sized soggy but still wriggling specimen under the collar, I slid in the barbed hook and pushed its body over the eye so that every spot of metal was hidden. I lobbed the rig into the fast water at the pool's top. It wafted downstream and then vanished into the depths.

Acute to the slightest pressure on the line, I waited. Nothing happened. I took a few more casts with the same result and thought of propping the pole on a stick like an old codger and dozing in the shade. The Schoharie was that kind of river. I took a final cast.

I was reeling in when my bail seized. The line drifted into a rocky shallows and snagged. Perplexed, I futzed with the gizmos controlling drag and line return, to no avail. Settling myself with a sigh, I unfolded my knife and started working the screws on either side of the bail. Because the knife had no screwdriver, I had to use a blade and found myself in danger of both stripping the screws and slicing a finger. After tinkering for thirty unpleasant minutes, the reel suddenly and mysteriously unclenched. There was a faint clunk and catch on each revolution, but it worked. I screwed the bail back in place and reversed the handle. Almost game, I nonetheless thought it best to leave that pool alone.

Onwards. I hazarded a dozen casts in pockets behind big stones where the creek narrowed, with no results. I quit fishing and lounged on a flat stone, reading *Ktaadn*, Thoreau's account of his expedition to the summit of the highest peak in Maine. Often distracted, I looked upriver and tried to console myself with a tidbit of Thoreau's philosophy. The great transcendentalist said that youth sought the woods for sport, but "at last, if [a man] has the seeds of a better life in him, he distinguishes his proper objects, as a poet or a naturalist it may be, and leaves the gun and fish-pole behind."

In *Ktaadn*, Thoreau briefly describes fishing before first light as his party approaches the peak. He dwells on none of the details, apparently gauging the emotions engendered as unworthy of his pen. A choice perhaps partially responsive to a brand of frontiersman literature, a large part of the ubiquitous journalist fodder of his day.

I must admit that I would rather read Hemingway than Thoreau, but as I read *Ktaadn* I admired the precision of detail—the way geography, economics, history, and botany are woven into a deceptively impersonal report. At the very end of the journal, I was surprised to see that the primitive remoteness of the Maine woods rattled Thoreau. As I read I had the feeling that he'd rather be back at Walden Pond—suburban then as now.

While I was so absorbed, the afternoon reached its zenith and dwindled toward evening. I considered turning back but instead continued upstream. The sun had slipped behind gray and yellow cumulus collapsing in a brackish sky. I came to an oblong pool fronted by a grassy berm. The clouds ruptured, and the sun slid forth. I stripped and waded gingerly in the glassy water, which was cold but not frigid, already starting to warm.

After dunking several times, mightily pleased, I spread my clothes on the bank and sat lotus-like, letting the sun work on me. I closed my eyes and breathed deeply. Soon, I started to float. I opened my eyes. A small trout leapt in the shallows. The sun hummed. I closed my eyes. A black obelisk spun on its axis until it appeared as a cylinder, like a microfilm casing. The casing atomized and there was nothing except a colorless glow. On a far border I heard leaves crackling and a whistle. A golden pup shot from the woods and frolicked around my face.

A man emerged in the pup's wake. He seemed rattled to find a half-clothed apparition pointing a camera at his pet as it scrambled up and down the bank and splashed in the shallows. When he discovered I was a journalist from Woodstock and not some flipped-out yogi, he relaxed. He was Larry Kolbmann, a carpenter who lived above Silver Spring Ranch, originally from Philadelphia. He was in his early forties and had thinning hair and a muscular build. While chatting we threw sticks into the deep part of the pool, urging Sascha to fetch them. A rambunctious five-month-old, she galloped in shoulder-deep and balked just short of the final plunge.

"Fetch it! Sascha, fetch it!" We goaded her, much amused.

Emerging from the water, sopped and muddy, Sascha shook herself—dousing my camera, pad, and clothes—then deliriously dashed up and down the bank. Kolbmann reined her in, delighted to pose for the camera.

"At last. We're gonna make the big time," he said.

Kolbmann was driving down to Philly that night and pushed off. I gathered my things and tromped another mile up the valley, unimpressed by the angling prospects but entranced by the beauty of the stream. The sound of passing cars increased. I cut back to the road through fields, only a couple hundred yards' distance; An hour of fast walking and I was back at the car. Light poured in slabs over Plateau Mountain. I decided to give the Schoharie a final try, stowed my gear in the trunk, and let the car idle a moment before heading toward Hunter.

Passing through town I noticed that *Hunt for Red October* was playing the Orpheum, the next show due to start in five minutes. I hesitated, remembered Blake's proverb "He who desires but acts not, breeds pestilence," parked, and bought a five-dollar ticket.

The Hunter Orpheum was petite, ragged, a bit seedy, and half full. A young couple flanked an elderly woman. A large man in woodsman's boots lounged in one of the wings placidly munching popcorn while four boys, who appeared to be his charges, played musical chairs to an unheard melody. There were no teenagers on dates.

Ten minutes late, the lights dimmed. I watched enthralled as Sean Connery paced his vessel through ocean canyons, playing hide-and-seek with the wolfpack. The technical accomplishment of the movie was ravishing and entertaining to a point—an expensive-looking woman, wearing nothing but jewels, juggling peas. Connery's submarine, silently propelled, surfacing rarely, the apogee of form, reminded me of the wiliest of fish—trout. I sat watching, immersed in an exciting meditation on the relationship between submarines, trout, and worms—linked through their "underness."

Most worms seemed to me fairly innocuous (discounting the 100-foot nemerteans, various parasitic, leechlike worms that suck vitality from their hosts, and the carniverous eely annelids with razor-sharp teeth and poison fangs). As for submarines and trout, I decided subterfuge was in their natures. Herodotus mentions subs, as does da Vinci. Men have always been quick to see their military and scientific application. The first subs, made of leather, used a giant hand drill to try to puncture hulls.

After the movie I decided to eat Mexican food (another "under"). By the time I'd finished, it was nearly midnight. I crossed the deserted street to the car and noticed no moon or stars in the sky. The air chilled; it was April again. Reaching under the front seat on the passenger's side, I checked my bait. The cooler temperatures had invigorated the crawlers. They danced through my fingers, naked and swift.

I drove the empty midnight road through Stony Clove, Lanesville, and Chichester. At Phonecia I turned west and stopped at a spot I know. The Esopus coursed beneath me. Headlights flashed sporadically on the highway above. I assembled my rod and tried to accustom my eyes to the dark. Inching forward, I felt my way down to the river's edge.

Next to the water it was clammy. Mist rose off the viscous blackness that swept my feet. I shivered. Closing my eyes, I reached for the rod tip, found the monofilament and followed it to the hook, which I put between my lips. Its small barbs pushed into my flesh. I took a crawler from the cup. It popped in my hand like a whip.

I felt a crazy surge of hope as I cast, a blind conjurer, playing by feel. The bait disappeared, and line stripped off the reel. I tripped the bail and tensed, imagining the worm squiggling in the black flux. A shadow mass, a dull glint, launched like a torpedo from its perch—vicious, single-minded, and strong.

But nothing rose to my living charm. As I reeled in, I realized that my line had inexorably snarled. I tried to read the knots like braille, but it was no use; I cut it at its root. Then I climbed carefully up the rocky bank, walked quickly back along what, coming down, had been indistinct and had now become an obvious path, and drove home.

The first thing I did after coming in was stash the leftover worms in the fridge. I sat in the living room and drank a large glass of water. I lathered my hands and scrubbed them a long time under a warm tap. Then I got into bed. As I drifted off, I felt myself borne on a crib of black water. Soon it would be summer. On damp evenings the nightcrawlers would appear palpitating and engorged on the bluestone steps still warm from the heat of day. I saw the crawlers casting themselves forward like empty sleeves. I saw their blind tips nuzzling upward. Cicadas sizzled; a bullfrog chimed. And as my hand opened, I felt the tubes of cool purple flesh dive off my fingers, back into the gaping ground.

BEHIND HUTCHIN HILL

1

I GREW UP ON TOP of Hutchin Hill, and the back country beyond the Hyatts and Maynard Keefe's woodlots will always have a special significance to me. The bowl beneath Sugarloaf Mountain, the spur off Twin's face, and the clear stream running down from the cull called Pecoy Notch were the scene of many boyhood jaunts.

As I grew older I began to fix my sights on the high places, so I set out to explore the mountains in earnest, taking long circuits to the summits and bushwhacking down the spurs. The urge to climb, to go deep in the woods, to sit on the mountaintop built up in me and tightened like a knot.

These expeditions were solitary and silent. After several years I began walking without compass, food, or canteen, using only water from springs and streams as sustenance. Those days in the mountains were an attempt to separate myself from a world that in one way or another tried to tell me how to live my life.

Now when I think of what I was about—half starved,

an ache in my navel like a branding iron spiked to the groin—I realize that I was only trying to prove myself worthy. I was drawn to the life of the hermit, the monk; I instinctively gleaned how those men turn isolation into an art. Taking the long view, however, I always wanted to return to the world of family and friends and to the worldly pursuits that even then had sunk their claws into my being.

René Daumal in *Mount Analogue*, an unfinished jewel of a book written in the '40s and recently reissued, writes: "You cannot stay on the summit forever; you have to come down.... So why bother in the first place? Just this: What is above knows what is below, but what is below does not know what is above."

My thoughts exactly.

2

Like all knowledge (or ways of seeing) mountaineering must be practiced; memory ossifies and distorts. It had been too long since my last real hike—a June ramble to the top of Westkill Mountain. Soon after, I had sprained one ankle and then the other. I spent the summer hobbling around, motor-touring through Delaware County.

By mid-October, I was suffocating. Throngs of tourists flowed across Woodstock's streets as though they had just stepped off an escalator. They goggled at the wonder world of autumn foliage and the quaint, enticing shops. Route 212 from Zena to Bearsville was congested with traffic.

One ankle still tender, I nevertheless decided to climb into the back country. I brought my Daumal, a pad, a camera, a bagel and cream cheese, an anjou pear, a bottle of seltzer water, two extra shirts, spare socks, matches, and a book of poems by Janine Vega. My plan was simple:

to reach the top of Twin by early afternoon, sprawl on a rocky outcrop, take in the view, read a little, write, shoot some photos, and cool out.

Parking on top of Hutchin Hill, I started out. It was a warm mid-October day. Autumn storms had hit the Catskills hard in recent days. Water coursed off the mountainside. I tromped along, head full of static.

The road I walked once connected the homestead of Doc Hasbrouck to the outside world. Romain Wilber, age seventy, has lived most of his life a mile downstream from the old Hasbrouck place. He remembers Doc as a short stocky fellow who kept two oxen.

Each spring Doc hitched oxen to his wagon and rode to town; winters he was snowed-in. Wilber remembers a potato patch behind Doc's house. Discussing nineteenth-century life on the backside of Hutchin Hill, Wilber said, "You either died of starvation or hard work."

I walked along the old road, marveling that it was still in such good shape. Half a day's work with the oxen and you could almost drive to Hasbrouck's front door. I looked (with a wonder I never cease to feel) at the stone wall skirting the roadside—a single-minded frenzy of labor.

I pictured Hasbrouck coming home as an old man, back to his place, back to the life he had chosen. He had known it would be rough but took it anyway. He was always carrying something; was never empty-handed. There was no phone and little mail. He kept accounts by kerosene lamp. Wood was always burning. The smell of smoke worked itself deep into his clothes and skin. When they put him in the ground he had these mountains in his blood.

Water sluiced over the broken road. I came to a place of flat red stones, freshets flowing smooth as silk. Ice crystals clung to the splayed rootwork of an upturned tree. What Wilber called Terry Creek sounded near. I ducked under a deadfall and marked the subtle impression of human hands on the streamside contours.

At the old homestead, hunters and campers have left their mark. What might have been Hasbrouck's kitchen floor was a cache of shattered glass and rusted beer cans full of bullet holes. Several firepits have been gagged with trash.

I mulled over what had been disturbing me on the way down. The Dalai Lama had just been awarded the Nobel Peace Prize. His response to the event seemed ludicrous. "I'm just a simple Buddhist monk," said the priest-king. This from a man who jets around the world, lives in regal style, and is deified by millions of subjects.

Shucking it off, I bushwhacked upstream. The woods were quiet and clear. My spirits leavened as I tromped, scattering the little forest creatures from their lays with the news: *the woodsman approaches!* Sugarloaf's steep wall rose before me, balsam crowned. A mile from the foundation site the stream split. I broke the walk and photographed the fork. Starting up the larger branch, I questioned whether I had chosen correctly. The last time I had gone that way I found myself high on Twin's flank. The right fork was up to its old tricks. It veered from the notch, rising sharply. Skittering down a steep bank I found the stream's first basin: a pellucid pool sunk in a rocky cleft. I sat a while listening to water and the wind rattling bare trees.

It was getting on toward noon. I began moving again, stomping up a high bank and making tracks through a forest of mature maple. A chipmunk shot from under my feet, a whisk of auburn fur. The nape of my neck prickled. The chipmunk scampered up a tree and disappeared into a hole the size of my fist. Cautiously, I approached. Curling from the den's roof were white mushrooms sprouting like delicate fingers from a child's upturned palm. The chipmunk's twitching nose and wet black eyes peeped; spying me, he flipped out of sight. Every minute or two he'd pop out only to find me pointing a camera at him. The clicking shutter sounded like a miniature guillotine.

Soon I arrived at the notch. Terry Creek was furred with moss, and its velvety green glowed against the ocher and umber forest floor and grays of sugar-maple and beech. From a percussive clap at Hasbrouck's place, the stream's timbre had tuned to a tinkle of Japanese delicacy. Steep walls of broken rock rose to ledges and spurs. The giddy heights of the mountain face pressed relentlessly downward or wavered overhead, ethereal. I creeped forward, stopping to fix my footing and steady my breath. The stream ducked underground as I ascended, a flicker deep beneath my feet.

Maynard Keefe said fifty years ago his father Herb and Freddie MacDaniel used to travel this route to snag wayward cows that had wandered from their Woodstock farms to Platteclove. Keefe said that Catskill cows, adept mountaineers, were always climbing over the passes to what they must have hoped were greener pastures. The Greene County farmers would obligingly barn the Ulster farmers' heifers. Keefe and MacDaniel would start from Keefe Hollow at five a.m. and arrive in Elka Park by 9:30, in time for breakfast at Burn's Tavern. Listening to gossip over pancakes and eggs, they'd learn who'd barned their stock, and the cows would be driven home by dogs superb at their job. It must have been a lark for the two men— friends and rivals, cagy, hard, and spry—taking off on a day's journey to reclaim their cows. I see them crossing the Sawkill in first light; by sunrise, near the old Hasbrouck place; at seven, making tracks up this notch that few since have cared to negotiate.

As I picked my way along with the help of a walking stick, I imagined what I might look like from above: a tiny figure crawling over rough terrain, pausing often, my progress fitful. I climbed 500 feet in half an hour, coming into the thin saddle that sits at 2,700 feet between Sugarloaf and Twin.

Two backpackers gazed earnestly at the Department of Environmental Conservation trail signs. They introduced themselves as Simon Kelemen, age thirty-seven, from Clinton, New Jersey, and Bill Haynes, age thirty-eight, from Perkasie, a suburb northwest of Philadelphia. Simon, whose self-deprecating manner I found endearing, said he had three kids. "They're a herd. It's nice to not have to worry about anyone's bodily functions but my own."

Simon worked as a chemist for Exxon, trying to figure out how to dissolve the tar balls besotting Prince William Sound. Both men, longtime backpacking companions, had a history of hiking in the Catskills. Bill and I ragged on Simon about his job as Bill cleaned a knee that he had gashed in a fall coming down Sugarloaf's south side.

"I wrote the governor a letter a while back complaining there was no place in the Catskills you could go on a quiet night and not hear a truck," said Bill, wincing as antiseptic sizzled in his wound.

I said that I'd meet them on top of Twin and took off. In some places the trail was nearly vertical. I pulled myself over rocks, occasionally catching faint sounds from below of Bill and Simon. I didn't envy them their full packs. I fabricated a little ditty to keep my spirits up: "Chickenheart! Chickenheart! Chickenheart! Ho! Chickenheart! Chickenheart! Chickenheart! No! Him has bear heart! Wolf heart! Ram heart! Go! Chickenheart! Chickenheart! Chickenheart! Ho!" Puff, puff, gasp, puff, gasp, cough, spit, gasp, puff, repeat (etc.).

After a brutal forty minutes, I reached the 3,500-foot summit and plopped myself down on a rocky outcrop. A thick haze obscured the far distance. My pear had gotten mashed in the pack, but I ate it anyway, along with the bagel and drank a fair portion of my water. Then I opened my Daumal:

> When you strike off on your own, leave some trace of your passing which will guide you coming back: one stone set on another, some grass flattened by a blow of your stick. But if you come to an impasse or a dangerous spot, remember that the trail you left could lead people coming after you into trouble. So go back along your trail and obliterate any traces you have left. This applies to anyone who wishes to leave some mark of his passage in the world. Even without wanting to, you always leave a few traces. Be ready to answer to your fellow men for the trail you leave behind you.

I looked down the spur leading to what Wilber calls "Beech Bone" and Keefe calls "Bear's Head." I had toyed with the idea of casting off the summit and bushwhacking down this spur, but it was late afternoon and I didn't feel up to it. Bill and Simon arrived, threw off their packs, and sprawled on the rocks. Both men seemed worried about water and finding a place to camp, and Bill complained about the haze. He was angry at the mountains for his knee, so I gave him the Daumal to read, pointing out this particular passage:

> If you slip or have a minor fall, don't allow yourself an instant's pause. Find your pace again the moment you get up. In your mind take careful note of the circumstances of your fall, but don't let your body linger over what happened. The body constantly tries to draw attention to itself by its shiverings, its breathlessness, its palpitations, its shudders and sweats and cramps; but it reacts quickly to any scorn and indifference in its master. Once it senses that he is not taken in by its jeremiads, once it understands that it will inspire no

pity for itself that way, then it comes into line and obediently accomplishes its task.

Bill handed the book back without comment.

I tried to keep reading, but the page swam before my eyes. Spreading an extra shirt on the ground, I announced that I intended to nap. Drifting off I heard voices. I opened my eyes to find two more men had entered the clearing, visiting for the day from Connecticut. The lean one, with dark hair and a walking stick with a carved bird on top, started in about Lyme disease. "This place is lousy with deer. They use the trail. Their droppings are everywhere. I picked a tick off my clothes on the way up here."

The clouds had molten edges, and the haze a yellowish sheen. I drifted off as the four men chattered. Half asleep, I felt something crawling in my hair above my eyes; I brushed it away and conked out as the two parties went their separate ways—Bill and Simon down towards Indian Head and Echo Lake and the two Connecticut daytrippers back to Elka Park.

The wind glided over the mountaintop. "Fallen Angel," Robbie Robertson's anthem for Richard Manual, ran through my mind. A bird perched on my third eye: I saw wings pressed tight against its body, the thin beak curved. A diffuse presence hovered in the notch; one hawk and then another broke silently from a rocky outcrop into the haze.

I righted myself, feeling logy, my ankle stiff. A film seemed to cover my retinas, which I rubbed and rubbed to no avail. I headed down the trail noticing how the walking stick had left its fangs in the gray rock. It took an hour to descend. Approaching the cull, I heard more voices and spied a couple gamboling through the woods. They veered toward Elka Park. I wanted to scream. In the days I used to frequent the Twin-Indian Head Range it was rare to see one person—let alone six—in the space of a short afternoon. The mountains felt despoiled, their wilderness gone. The solitude I had found so precious, which had meant so much to me, was compromised.

As I moved deeper into the notch, the anger faded. I realized that the slow, trying descent had rattled me. Underlying each step was concern for my ankle. Where the stream sprung from the rocks I paused and drank, plunging my face in a mossy pool. I entered gentler country and found myself singing.

3

Last night I went out walking beneath the full moon at one in the morning. Today at sunset I decided to head back into the mountains to finish this. Once again, I park at the top of Hutchin Hill and head up the 2,500-foot peak called Bear's Head (Keefe), Beech Bone (Wilber) or left nameless (by half a dozen maps).

In the west the sky flares. I move quickly through a birch forest in the dimming light, following an old logging road through last summer's nettles, berry bushes, and scrub. Black birch grow up in its middle. I break off a twig and gnaw it. Sweet sassafras spurts, not as fragrant as April.

I know the way, having climbed to the top of this mountain often. En route, I have never seen another person, although there are signs: fifteen years ago Keefe had the mountain logged; hunters have built cave shelters on top; there is evidence that the wide rock shelves and sinks were quarried. Huge bluestone slabs stand upended. Each must weigh over a ton.

By the time I reach the penultimate plateau the woods are murky. The gap between this digit of the Twin-Indian Head Range and the southern ranges fifteen miles distant feels full of space and wind. The dull platinum glow of Copper Lake looms far below me as do the lights of Mink

Hollow. If this mountaintop has been lumbered, it was long ago. The stand of maple, beech, and oak is big and old, the ground a mosaic of worn stone.

When I used to come here with the dog, he'd go wild, sniffing the rock ledges and pawing the musty earth beneath the overhangs. Driving down the mountain one August, I saw a bear a mile from where I'm standing. I thought it was a huge black dog until I saw him move. As he barreled down the road, I clocked him at over 30 mph, back haunches high and churning. He catapulted off the roadside into the sticks and went crashing away as I slammed to a halt and jumped out, breathless and elated.

This evening the forest thrums. I cross the plateau and head up the final rise. I climb slowly and steadily, sometimes using my hands, careful of my ankle. I remember this is a land of skews and cants, splintered ground, and a honeycomb of holes.

I skirt a brim of flat rocks around the cap-shaped summit. Two decades ago the rock-oak and scrub birch below the cliffs were shorter and the view better. A stunted birch has plied into the rock shelf; I climb it and perch in a socket of branches. The tree pitches in the gusting wind, which comes from the northwest—a clear, cold wind sweeping across Winnipeg and Saskatchewan, Manitoba and Moosenee, Thunder Bay and Sioux Lookout, Huron, and Sault Sainte Marie. It rakes my cheeks and ears, and my eyes tear when I face it full. I slide to the ground. Urinate. Retie my boots, ready myself, then work slowly down the mountain. Sitting often, I slosh through dead leaves, loose soil, and shifting rock. It's very dark and I feel my way by instinct. The climb has put my forebrain to sleep.

Suddenly, jet shadows melt to mercury. An eerie iridescence sweeps the forest floor. Hunched, I turn and peer over my left shoulder. There, above the summit, the full moon has broken from clouds. I inadvertently give a cry of acknowledgment and recognition. Maniacally grinning, alone in the wild night with the crackling trees, I summon that which makes me most deeply happy and afraid.

I negotiate the steep descent effortlessly and without mishap. I am one with the night woods in the place that means more to me than anywhere else on earth—each heartbeat homage, each breath drenched with the rushing clouds and the rising moon.